T0154847

Tommy Adkins

At Home and Abroad

RMP
River Market Press

Tommy Adkins

At Home and Abroad

by

Frederick French

Corporal Chevron, RE

Edited and with a Foreword by
Cynthia A. Nahrwold, PhD
University of Arkansas at Little Rock

River Market Press Editorial Board: Charles M. Anderson, George Jensen, Joanne Matson, Cynthia Nahrwold.

Manuscript Editor: Cynthia Nahrwold
Interior Design: Charles Anderson and Jade Fitch
Drawings: Frederick French
Cover Design: Priscilla Rodriguez
Editorial Assistants: Trent Kays and Phillip Garcia
Technical Support: Jennika Smith

ISBN

The front cover photograph is the only surviving image of Frederick French in service. Its location is unknown. He is the soldier farthest left, leaning against the bridge railing.

Tommy Adkins at Home and Abroad is set in Minion Pro and Georgia using Adobe InDesign 5.5 and Photoshop 5.5. Cover Fonts include American Captain, Market Deco, and Super Retro m54.

River Market Press is a press imprint of the Department of Rhetoric and Writing at the University of Arkansas at Little Rock. Affiliated with Moon City Press and The University of Arkansas Press, River Market Press is dedicated to the production of quality nonfiction books, especially first books by new authors. Its educational mission is to help graduate and undergraduate students to learn and to participate in the full process of publishing books, from acquisition of manuscripts to book design and production.

Copyright information Here

Contents

Editor's Foreword   vii

Preface   xii

Dedication   xv

Prologue   xvii

Chapter 1: Soldier of the King   1

Chapter 2: Deciding to Desert the Army   7

Chapter 3: My Third Enlistment   17

India	22
Venereal Diseases	27
War	28
Mesopotamia	42
The Capture of Basra	47
The Port of Basra	56
The Battle for Kurna	59
Gurmit Ali	66
Nasiriyeh	73
Kut	89
On Leave	98
Back with the Fighting Forces	104
Homeward Bound	116

Appendices

Appendix A: Frederick French's Certificate of Naturalization

Appendix B: Original Manuscript Pages

Appendix C: Army Discipline

Appendix D: Glossary

Editor's Foreword

The histories . . . are all written out by "big bugs," Generals and renowned historians, and like the fellow who called a turtle a "cooter," being told that no such word as cooter was in Webster's dictionary, remarked that he had as much right to make a dictionary as Mr. Webster or any other man; so have I to write a history.

Sam Watkins, *Company Aytch*

Watkin's account of his Civil War experiences as a Confederate private stands out among memoirs because of its being written by a member of the ranks—someone who wouldn't have been expected to use words to communicate wit, humor, cynicism, horror.

The same can be said of Frederick French, author of *Tommy Adkins*, which records French's WWI experiences as a member of the British Expeditionary Force.

If French kept a journal—he doesn't say, so we don't know, but given all the direct quotations, he must have, or he had a wonderful memory, or he had, like Watkins, a way with words. Journal or no journal, French gives us an engaging memoir, despite his claim that he was "no writer" (from his Preface) and that he was writing *Tommy Adkins* under the pressure of friends.

We know a bit about him prior to his first enlistment. His maternal side is from Essex, a part of southeast England known as East Anglia. We know, according to his Full Service Record, that at the time of his first enlistment (1908), he was almost 22 years old (21 years, 11 months). However, in one section of his memoir, he notes that in 1910 he had been in the service for three years, which means that he enlisted in 1907. Thus, we could infer that he was born in 1886 (although a note elsewhere in his personal papers says he was born in 1884).

Some of this discrepancy might be attributed to his 1910 change of last name from Cadosch to French via a "deed poll," a legal document allowing an individual to abandon his former name and use his new name from that time on. Either before or after this time (yet still in 1910), French assumed the name of Jack Jones from Cardiff, Wales—a change noted in his memoir—thus allowing him to reinlist under his assumed name while still enlisted under his legal name.

We also know, according to his Full Service Record, that French was "discharged physically unfit February 21, 1919." (The illness leading up to that discharge is detailed in his memoir.) And according to military records, French received several medals: the 1914 Star (in 1915) and the Victory Medal and British War Medal in 1921.

After that time, we hear nothing of French—until his date of naturalization to the United States: December 14, 1944. (See Appendix A for a copy of his naturalization certificate, acquired from family members.) And we don't know when he wrote his memoir. (He had to have written it before 1951, the year of his death.) As noted above, we don't know if he kept a journal. (With Sam Watkins, we know that he didn't "propose to make . . . a connected journal, for I write entirely from memory. . . .") But how could French keep all these stories, this dialogue, these quotes in his head for years?

And what quotes. His first night in the Army, French meets a soldier with two medals. Asking what the medals were for, French gets this explanation, which he records with a straight face *a la* Buster Keaton:

> Ah, young man, I'm very proud of these medals. You can only get these on very special occasions. This one was awarded to me for making Army puddings. All soldiers like lots of pudding, so one year the King had more soldiers than he needed, so he told me to give them plenty of pudding, with the result that they all got sick and died. You see, they were suffering from puddingitis. This other medal is called the Bethlehem Star. It was given to me by the Shah of Persia. One day when he was over here, trying to count all the guns we have, he had a little sack full of these stars; they're supposed to be lucky and work the magic charm of turning water into wine, but it didn't work in this country.

On Day One, French meets a soldier who believes that he's not valued, that he can, in fact, be gotten easily rid of if necessary. Here French meets a soldier whose cynicism suggests that British security is so lax that any potential enemy could infiltrate the lines. Finally, no wine. Blast. . . .

Later on (and more humorously), French admits to his lack of coordination regarding foot drill and rifle exercises—and the consequent response of his instructors:

> We were then split into squads and sections and marched to the parade grounds to go through the monkey motions called foot

drill. In a few days I got to abhor those drills; at each command or order, I'd very often go the wrong way to the displeasure of the instructor. If he said "right turn," I was bound to go left. The instructor, who was about 50 yards in front of the squad, would come for me at the double and put his face so close to mine that I thought he was going to kiss me. Instead, he said,

"What the hell is the matter with you? Don't you know your right from your left?" He'd then grab hold of my shoulders and jerk me 'round to the right. "That's your right." He then switched me to the left. "Now, you blithering idiot," he hollered, "keep that in your thick noodle; next time you go wrong, into the awkward squad you go." . . . The next parade, we spent an hour in going through rifle exercises, usually winding up with more trouble for me. In trying to slope arms, I'd often drop the rifle with a bang on the ground, and I often found it difficult to stick the bayonet on the top of the rifle, which would cause a lot of merriment amongst my comrades and a lot of cursing from the instructor; he called me all the funny names I'd never heard before. I suppose they were military terms which didn't appear in the Bible. . . .

Many times during the editing of this memoir, I burst out laughing. In the following excerpt, French is in Bombay with his pals Jack and Peter. Thinking they'll be all right—despite the fact they'd finished off a bottle of whiskey—French leaves them on their own. Listen to Jack and Peter. Better yet, read the following passage aloud:

"Come on, you damn son of a Norfolk farmer; let's go and see something," said Peter. "This are war will all be over before we get there an' this is the first war and the last war I was ever in, and I don't want it ta finish too quickly 'cos I want ta handle a lot more of these thirty rupee stunts. Talk about the Army: 'Come on boys, join the Army; it's a damn good Army.'"

"For crissake, what the hell is the matter with you?" said Jack. "You're talking about a good Army."

"It's the first time I heard you say that; you said last week that this Army was no damn good. Yes you did, so don't deny it, the way yer throwing yerself about 'cause you got a few marbles in yer pocket. Anybody would think you was some unpaid adjunct or something. I moves to crack the Army up and to hell with the Army," said Peter. "Come on, and let's forget we're in the blooming Army for a few hours. Anyhow, we got till tomorrow morning before we join the Army again, so let's go and see if we can drop a few bombs on Bombay."

Although I've read this and other passages in which French captures Peter's Cockney accent—French even attempts to phonetically record Industani in other sections of his memoir—I still laugh.

But I'm not laughing *at* anyone—especially not Frederick French. I'm laughing *with* him as he injects humor into the story of his enlistments—a story that could have been *so* boring but wasn't. For a man who said he was "no writer," he certainly was.

Because of French's innate ability to tell a story and to tell it well, both the hilarious and the horrible sides of war (the latter downplayed somewhat, as many veterans do—"all in the life of a soldier," French says), my number one priority as an editor was to keep his voice, keep his style. What you read here is the writing of a British private (later corporal) from London's working class. His voice, not my voice. As many of you reading these words know, resisting the urge to fiddle with someone else's writing is easier said than done. Someone serving as an editor always (it seems) wants to impose his or her own word choice or way of formulating a sentence on the work on another. Doing so is easy. Why? Because no one has ever taught people how to edit; instead, they are merely *told* to edit—with no boundaries set around that editing, with no level of edit stipulated. Only through full-time professional experience as a technical editor did I learn how to maintain a level of edit. I was *taught* how to do so. "If the change you want to make doesn't significantly improve the material, don't make the change." That was and still is my mantra, one that helped me tremendously in editing *Tommy Adkins*.

And I needed all the help I could get. I started off with a scanned copy of a manuscript—see Appendix B for several pages of that manuscript—one with apparently two introductions and two Chapter 1s. What should I use where? Having read through the manuscript (handwritten in pencil on the front and back sides of lined notebook paper grown fragile with age) I made my best guess, knowing I could always go back and move sections around. One of the introductions became the book's Prologue. One of the Chapter 1s became Appendix C devoted to the topic of Army discipline. I believe I did make my best guess, for without realizing it until I'd finished editing—truly!—the book's beginning and ending echo each other:

Beginning: "Stoney broke and alone in London."
Ending:
> ". . . and I found myself once again alone in
> London as I'd been some 15 years before,
> stoney broke and out of a job."

Another challenge I faced was the difference in language. Yes, what French wrote and what I write are both English. But what I speak and write is 21st-century American English; what he spoke and wrote is 19th-century British Empire English. A hundred years separates our word choice, our colloquialisms, our idioms, our military terms. American word processing programs constantly flag British spellings (e.g., "colour," "maneuvre," "prioritise") as if they were incorrect. Ignoring such flags was easy for me. What wasn't so easy was tracking down the meanings of so many words and phrases that were new to me. What's a Sam Browne belt? "Kick over the traces"—what's the meaning of that phrase? An ADC is _____? What's half a crown worth in American money? (Look at the glossary—Appendix D—and you'll find the answers to these and many other questions.) Tracking down the answers to my questions took more than a bit of time, more than a few sources (both print and electronic). But doing so was *fun*—and has resulted in my having at my disposal so many new words and terms and meanings. Now I know that a "babu" is a Hindu clerk literate in English. A "yard square" is the British equivalent of "square yard" in American English. "Half a crown" is 50 cents American money. A "rupee" is the basic unit of Indian currency; at the time of WWI, 15 rupees equaled 1 British pound. (The phrase "shy pilot" was also new to me, and I had no idea what it meant. Go to the glossary and prepare to be surprised.)

Then return to the text of French's memoir and continue to be surprised. Coming to this book, you probably thought that a World War I memoir would be set in France—on the Western Front, no doubt. Instead, French takes us to India and Mesopotamia. He provides us with his own handdrawn maps of certain areas, artistic renditions of an Arab sheik (or "sheikh" as he spells it), stories of battles you've never heard of.

French gives us a view of the Great War that few have seen. For that, I thank him.

Cynthia A. Nahrwold
March 2013

Preface

This book has been written under the pressure of friends. I have avoided putting this together for several reasons as I'm no writer. I hate writing, especially about experiences which may or may not be interesting, and my vocabulary is very limited. But having quite a lot of time on my hands at present, here it is, and you may have it for what it's worth.

In this book, I have tried to describe the life of a private soldier, better known to the world as Tommy Adkins of the British Army at home, on active service, in peace time, and on foreign service in some part of the great Empire. If this doesn't meet all your demands, please don't criticize too harshly because after all I'm only a common private, Tommy Adkins, of the rank and file—at your service.

Most of the names of the higher ranks, no doubt, will be familiar to you; for obvious reasons, some of the names are purely fictitious. But I honestly say that the details are absolutely true as far as my memory goes.

Frederick French

Dedication

To the ladies of Rangoon, Bombay, and Calcutta, this book is dedicated for their kindness to the boys of Indian Expeditionary Force "D" who went to Mesopotamia in 1914 to take part in the World War.

Prologue

"March the prisoner in."

A soldier between an armed escort was marched into the centre of a battalion of soldiers formed up in U formation on the barrack square of one of the King's military stations not far from London. He had been court-martialed, and the nature of his crime and the punishment awarded was being read out to his comrades by the adjutant of the regiment. The soldier between the escort had deserted His Majesty's Army and was sentenced to serve two years' imprisonment with hard labour and to be discharged from His Majesty's forces.

As I watched the proceedings and saw the soldier marched away to prison, I wondered what I should do. I was a newly enlisted man, just arrived to report myself at the barracks, and was still in my civilian clothes. But after watching the above scene, I had a feeling that I didn't want to be a soldier. What did I do? This story will tell you!

Chapter 1

Soldier of the King

Stoney broke and alone in London. That's how I found myself one day some years before the Great War. What a predicament to be in, not knowing where my next meal was coming from. I was one of those young fellows who never did trouble to look ahead. Why should I bother? I was possessed with all the best gifts that God could bestow on any person: strength and health.

I'd lost my job, and work at the time was very hard to find, especially in the country where I came from, so with a few pounds I came to London with the good intention of finding myself work. I'd never been in London before and was green to city life. I suppose I was a country bumpkin coming to town. Well, London looked mighty good to me for a day or two. I thought surely it was the place to land a job with lots of people all hustling to and fro, traffic everywhere, everybody seeming to be busy. Nicely dressed men and women, their nice clothes so different to my country-made suit. I did the rounds, applying here and there where I thought I stood a possible chance, but "No, not today," the same results from the employment offices with which London was flooded. I wondered how they maintained their places if they never had any jobs to offer, but all I got was "Come in again tomorrow." After several days, my patience finally got exhausted. I didn't know whether to return home. Anyhow, I decided to enjoy myself before deciding what to do; perhaps fate would do something, so I let myself go as far as my remaining finances would permit. I went to shows, music halls, most of the theatres including a chance meeting with some of the pretty London girls until my creditors refused any further embursements, and so there I was, face to face with nothing. I couldn't go home because I had no fare.

As I was walking slowly along the sidewalk in the vicinity of Trafalger Square, wondering what I should do, my eyes caught sight of a big poster outside of a large building, which read in large type, "Join the Army and become a man," followed by descriptions of good pay, free rations, hospitals, and medical attention. Then under the poster were all kinds of soldiers, some on horse and some on foot, all dressed up in their smart-looking uniforms. There were big dragoons, lancers, engineers, artillery with big guns, medical corps, infantrymen with rifles and all the rest of the British Army, including generals and majors all decked up in their pretty clothes.

As I stood there gazing at that poster, a soldier came to the doorway and beckoned to me: "Hello, young fellow! Want to join the Army? Come right in here and let me look you over." And before I had time to look around, he had pushed me into his office.

"Sit down," he said. Then he went on: "Ever been in the Army before?"

"No sir," I said.

"Well, it don't matter much if you was, only you don't have to tell me, understand?"

"Yes sir, I understand."

"And you don't have to call me Sir; you can save that for the officers. I'm only a recruiting sergeant, and my job is to get smart young fellows like you to join His Majesty's Army."

But I said, "I don't know anything about the Army. I never worked for the Army before."

"Don't worry about that, young man. You don't have to know anything in the Army. All you have to do is to obey orders and do as you're told; in fact, we teach you everything and give you nothing. I mean, we give you everything you want. We pay you, feed you, give you a gun to play with. When you're sick, we have nice hospitals, doctors, and pretty nurses to tuck you in at night. Now what more do you want? A gentleman's life, that's what it is, and what's more, if you happen to be alive at the end of twenty years, the King gives you a couple of pounds a week to get out of the Army and stay out. There, doesn't that sound pretty good? Retired pensioners, that's what they call it."

He kept rattling on all about the Army, talk which I didn't understand.

"Now, young man, come into this room and let me run the tape 'round you."

There I stripped and was measured, weighed, made to hop on one leg, then the other, went through a few more motions, and was pronounced fit. The recruiting sergeant got me to sign a few Army documents and told me to be there at ten o'clock the following morning to see the doctor, who would test my heart, and then it wouldn't be long before I was a full-blown soldier. With that, he gave me a shilling, took me to the canteen and filled me up with bread, cheese, and beer, told me where to sleep that night, and left me.

Frederick French

I spent my shilling in the canteen that night, drinking beer which I shared with a few soldiers who dropped in and seemed quite pleased to help me with my beer. One soldier had two medals, and I asked him what they were for.

"Ah, young man, I'm very proud of these medals. You can only get these on very special occasions. This one was awarded to me for making Army puddings. All soldiers like lots of pudding, so one year the King had more soldiers than he needed, so he told me to give them plenty of pudding, with the result that they all got sick and died. You see, they were suffering from puddingitis. This other medal is called the Bethlehem Star. It was given to me by the Shah of Persia. One day when he was over here, trying to count all the guns we have, he had a little sack full of these stars; they're supposed to be lucky and work the magic charm of turning water into wine, but it didn't work in this country."

Next morning the canteen man called me about seven o'clock and gave me a job to wash a few dishes and sweep the floor; for that he gave me my breakfast. At ten o'clock the recruiting sergeant came for me to get prepared for the doctor, who arrived about noon. I went through the same motions as the day before, was sworn in by taking the oath, and became a faithful soldier of the King, whom I was to serve for 12 years. The sergeant gave me half a crown and told me that the remainder of the day was a holiday. I was to report to him the following morning at ten when I'd be dispatched to the depot of my regiment.

"You're in the Army now," he said, "and are subject to military law." What that was, I didn't know. I went back to the canteen and helped to serve the food and beer. So far as I could see, the Army appeared to be all right up to now.

Next day, the sergeant took me to the railway station, got my ticket, gave me another half a crown and some papers in an official envelope, and told me to report myself to the sergeant in charge of the guard room at Warley barracks. He laughed and said he hoped to see me a full-blown general someday, but he said, "If you don't like the Army, come and see me, and I'll fix you up in some other regiment." I thought that offer was pretty good of him. With that, he said,"So long and good luck."

Soon I arrived at Warley barracks, which was only a few miles from the east side of London. It was getting dark, so I was told to find the storekeeper and get my bedding. After making numerous inquiries and searching several barrack rooms, I located the storekeeper, half drunk in the canteen.

"Hello, youngster," he greeted me. "Got any money? If not, you ain't getting no bedding tonight."

I protested. "The sergeant said you would give me my bedding."

"To hell with the sergeant. I'm sergeant of the bedding. Come and sit down, kid, and attack a couple o' pints o' beer, and you'll find that I can do yer quite a lot of little favours."

The storekeeper surely had a throat for beer; pint after pint he'd consume, and I couldn't move him until closing time.

"Come along with me, youngster; I'll put you in the storeroom for tonight and fix you up in the morning."

He opened the door and pushed me in, saying that he'd see me in the morning. With that, he closed and locked the door on the outside. It was dark in the room, but luckily I had a box of matches and could see stacks of little square mattresses and lots of blankets. Being tired, I curled up amongst them and fell into a sound sleep. Some hours later, I was awakened by the sound of a bugle. Soon afterwards the storekeeper appeared: "Hello, kid, had a good sleep?" He gave me my bedding and told me to take it to the recruits' room just across the way where I should find a corporal who would take care of me.

The room was a large one with about 30 beds each side with long tables down the centre and forms to sit on. That room was full of recruits. They were all busy making up beds and sweeping the room. Although it was very cold, all the windows were open, but the soldiers seemed happy: Some were whistling, others were trying their voices at singing the latest songs. At my appearance, they stood and stared for a moment, then greeted me with one long yell: "Come in, chum, and make yourself at home if you have come to stop." Then a trumpet sounded. There was another yell. Some half dozen of those men disappeared with buckets and trays to return in a few moments with steaming hot tea and bread. "Come on, rookie, and munch in," they called to me. There was bread and large cans of jam washed down with what was supposed to be tea but tasted as if somebody had been washing his socks in it. That I found out consisted of breakfast. After the meal was over, a corporal appeared and called out my name. He showed me a little slip of paper with my number, rank, and name printed upon it. He took me to the medical inspection room where I was again subject to an examination, which I found out was just a matter of routine; for new recruits, it seemed to me just a way to get acquainted with medical officers.

The best part of that day was taken up in getting rigged up with my uniform and necessaries. From the clothing stores to the tailor's shop to get fitted and alterations made. I was then issued with all the different articles that go to make a British soldier's outfit. I never had so many things before in all my life. The outfit consisted of the following: four suits, two khaki suits, one canvas suit, and one dress suit made of red material with a white collar and cuffs with blue trousers and red stripes, three woolen shirts, three pairs of woolen socks, two pairs of heavy boots, one pair canvas slippers, boot brushes, hair brush, comb, shaving brush and razor, cleaning brush and polish for brass work, one large overcoat, and lots of other gear for cleaning purposes. I began to wonder how I was going to take care of all that stuff. I didn't have to wonder very long because I soon found out that somebody else was taking care of it for me. Although my uniform had to be neatly folded up in a certain way and placed on a shelf over my bed cot, the other things were kept in a box which was placed at the foot of the bed. That same day, two pairs of my socks mysteriously disappeared. I was advised to buy a lock and keep the box locked up at all times. I was now in uniform, and although I was supposed to have been fitted, I didn't feel so very comfortable; when I looked down, I could see that my trousers looked more like a concertina, but I was told that for a small fee, the tailor would put that all right. My shoes, too, seemed a few sizes too large; the shoemaker, though, would exchange my new, big shoes for a slightly used pair which would be more comfortable. I found that I could get almost anything done for a small fee, but as I had no fee at that time, I had to be content to walk around looking something like a scarecrow. I found that wearing my three shirts helped to fill out my khaki jacket so it didn't look too bad, but I made up my mind that I'd have to give the tailor his little fee as soon as I could. For some reason or other, my size had been sort of overestimated, and it was up to me to pay for alterations. Oh, well, I suppose that's the way they have in the Army.

The following day, for the benefit of the last joined recruits, a sergeant gave us a lecture on the day's routine as laid down in the rules and regulations. He had us all seated 'round the tables, himself standing at the end and every now and then striking the table with his cane as though putting emphasis upon his words.

"Now, my lads, I want you to pay particular attention to what I'm going to tell you and to remember it because this lecture is given only once. This life that you're about to enter is all new to you and is quite altogether different from what you've been used to. Most of you have only just left your mother's apron strings, and the profession you've now entered upon isn't an easy one as you'll no doubt find out. It calls for pluck, strength, endurance, patience, and obedience. You've become part of that great fighting machine that holds the great British Empire together, and there will be times when you'll be called upon to use tact and initiative in cases of great importance and responsibility. And don't forget that obedience is one of the most important rules laid down. Obey all orders given by a superior officer; your complaints, if any, will always be heard after and justly dealt with. Now, get that well fixed into your heads."

At that point an officer entered the room, the sergeant shouted "Attention," saluted the officer, and reported "All present." The officer saluted back and said, "Carry on, Sergeant."

"This is what is known as an infantry depot. Here you'll be gradually trained into the making of a good all 'round soldier of the King. When you leave this depot, it will be to join your regiment in whatever particular part of the world it may be quartered. There you'll find friendship and comradeship seldom found elsewhere. And wherever you see the Union Jack flying, you're just as good as being in your own home, but your happiness partially depends upon yourself and your using a little sound judgment. No efforts have been spared to make the life of a British soldier happy whether it be at home or abroad. Everything has been done for you to lead strong and healthy lives. You're surrounded with all kinds of sports material which you're expected to use. A lot of your increases in pay entirely depends upon your efficiency, and only one way to do that is to safeguard your health; when your health fails, so does your efficiency, and automatically your pay drops. Temptations you'll find plenty, especially abroad, which once indulged in are very hard to break. Keep away from the native women with whom you come in contact; many a promising young soldier's career has been cut short through these women. My advice to you is to avoid them like poison. Contagious diseases caught from these women are 10,000 times worse than those contracted from European women. Another thing to avoid is their native intoxicating drink, which has a far different action upon the human body than what you have been used to. Don't think this is all bunk; it's perfectly true. I've seen this with my own eyes and is good sound advice which I hope you'll follow."

That was one of a series of lectures which often took place in the afternoons. Other lectures were on different subjects such as the advantages of the Army, care and management of the rifle, memorization of the names of the component parts, etc., what and what not to do in the face of enemy fire, and 101 other things all to do with the Army.

Chapter 2

Deciding to Desert the Army

There were about 200 of us recruits in that depot. Also quartered there were a battalion of His Majesty's guards, but they were quite apart from us. The only time we came in contact with them would be in the canteen, and sometimes some of them would stand and watch us going through our monkey motions on the parade ground. Army routine was very much the same day after day with the exception of Saturday and Sunday. Saturday was a kind of cleaning-up day: Rooms were scrubbed, windows were cleaned, fireplaces were polished. Some of us were employed carrying coal to the barrack rooms, sergeants' mess, officers' mess, library, recreation rooms, etc.—a job despised by every recruit. The day would start at six-thirty with the sound of a bugle. A corporal would shout, "Come on, shake a leg!" and would throw all the windows open. We then made our beds up into armchair fashion, washed and shaved, and woe betide the man who went on parade without shaving (even though there was no hot water for shaving in the Army). Breakfast at seven-fifteen, consisting of bread and butter, sometimes porridge, and sometimes a piece of liver washed down with a pint of muddy tea. Coffee was never served. Tables and forms were then scrubbed and placed outside to dry.

A bugle would then sound the quarter hour for parade. Every man had to be on parade five minutes before time. The sergeant would shout, "Fall in! Answer to your names or the names you go by!" He'd call the roll and report "present" or otherwise to the officer who had just arrived. The officer would then inspect every individual both front and rear, and it would be just too bad for the man who wasn't spic and span; a man may have forgotten to polish a couple of buttons, perhaps he had overlooked the backs of his shoes, or he had left a couple of hairs on his face, all of which were punishable by two or three days' extra fatigue or confinement to barracks. The officer would only say, "Take his name, Sergeant, and consider yourself a prisoner at large." After the parade was dismissed, the prisoner would be escorted to the orderly room, and his punishment meted out to fit the crime. It was little crimes like the above which used to stick in the craw of many a young recruit and was the cause of many taking French leave.

We were then split up into squads and sections and marched to the parade grounds to go through the monkey motions called foot drill. In a few days I got to abhor those drills; at each command or order, I'd very often go the wrong way to the displeasure of the instructor. If he said "right turn," I was bound to go left. The instructor, who was about 50 yards in front of the squad, would come for me at the double and put his face so close to mine that I thought he was going to kiss me. Instead, he said, "What the hell is the matter with you? Don't you know your right from your left?" He'd then grab hold of my shoulders and jerk me 'round to the right. "That's your right." He then switched me to the left. "Now, you blithering idiot," he hollered, "keep that in your thick noodle; next time you go wrong, into the awkward squad you go." After an hour of that, during which there was more time wasted in trying to place the men in the proper positions, we were allowed an hour's rest. The next parade, we spent an hour in going through rifle exercises, usually winding up with more trouble for me. In trying to slope arms, I'd often drop the rifle with a bang on the ground, and I often found it difficult to stick the bayonet on the top of the rifle, which would cause a lot of merriment amongst my comrades and a lot of cursing from the instructor; he called me all the funny names I'd never heard before. I suppose they were military terms which didn't appear in the Bible, but he couldn't help it. It's a way they had in the Army.

We then had to go to the gymnasium for an hour of physical work, and oh boy, what an hour that was. We were made to do everything that appeared to be impossible. One instructor had an Italian name, so we called him "Spaghetti." His orders used to come from his mouth like greased lightning; they were so fast that we very often misunderstood them and would go wrong. He'd flare up and call us all numbskulls, nincompoops, sons of imbeciles and make us gallop 'round the gym until we hadn't a leg to stand on. Then without any breathing time, he'd make us press up and down on our hands until we were entirely exhausted. Never shall I forget Army gyms. That sort of training might be good for some, but it never did appeal to me. It was as much as we could do to crawl back to our barrack rooms.

It was then dinner time, twelve o'clock. Some would go to the canteen for a drink of beer if they were lucky enough to have the money. Dinner consisted of beef stew, potatoes, and bread washed down with water; mutton was issued twice a week, and once a week, we had canned beef. The rations were good and wholesome but entirely inadequate to compensate for the amount of energy consumed: For instance, the one-hour gymnasium training was equal to a week's ordinary manual labour. I'm quite certain we weren't getting our full amount of rations as laid down in Army rules, but we had to take or leave it and remain mum. After dinner, we were allowed to make our beds down and rest until lecture time, which finished up the day's training. At four-thirty, tea and bread, sometimes a little jam, was served. That was the last meal of the day unless a soldier happened to be in funds; then he could go to the canteen or coffee shop and indulge in a little luxury for supper. For recreation, there was the library, well stocked with books, papers, and magazines. Billiards and other games were always in progress. Then there was the beer canteen with its vaudeville shows where cheap artists used to do a turn. Or a soldier could remain in his barrack room and ponder over what a good Army he was in until ten-fifteen when all lights were put out on the sound of the bugle.

I soon began to find out that barrack room life was not all beer and skittles. It wouldn't have been so bad if a soldier could live on fresh air, but it was a long time to go without eats from four o'clock until eight the following day. We used to get very hungry lots of times and were always on the lookout for ways and means of getting some money to satisfy our hunger. Some of the soldiers would sell their kit, such as socks, shirts, and boots; others, although decent and honest fellows on enlistment, would resort to thieving a comrade's kit and disposing of it to some buyer for the sake of a few pints of beer and something to eat. The consequence was that on pay day, very few of us were lucky if we had any pay coming to us. Every week the day before pay day, there was a kit inspection. Every soldier was required to lay out his kit on his bed cot and was checked off by an officer. All deficiencies were replaced with a new kit and had to be paid for by the soldier concerned, with the result that we were more often than not always in debt to the government. We were getting one shilling a day, about 25 cents American money; out of that pay there were compulsory stoppages, such as a barber's fee at two pennies a month, three pennies a day for extra rations, which we seldom saw for so very little money came our way. I used to lie awake at night and wonder how I was going to stick it out for another 12 years.

It was always a mystery where our rations used to disappear, but the longer a soldier was in the Army, he soon began to see through the various channels of disappearing tricks.

There was the quartermaster, an officer who did the direct business with the contract butcher of purchasing the meat. Nothing prevented him from signing for 800 pounds of meat and getting only 600, the difference being split between him and the contractor. Then on the way to the cook house, it was possible to meet the wife of some sergeant; nothing was more easy than accidentally dropping a couple of pounds or so of meat, which would amount to the cost of a few pints of beer. Then there was the master cook to be taken into consideration; he always needed a few free drinks. Next to him were his cooks. Those fellows always had plenty of money to buy beer with although they were common soldiers like ourselves, so we could see quite plainly what portion of our rations used to land on our tables. Lost through shrinkage in cooking was one good excuse offered on some occasions. Some soldier had been plucky enough to complain, but complaints usually went up in smoke, and more than likely the complainer would be punished for making a frivolous complaint.

Now there was the corporal who used to run the mess booth. It was his duty to buy the extras that we paid three pennies a day for. He and the canteen managers were always the best of pals, and by the time those two had finished juggling with our funds, there was very little left of our extra rations. So much for the British Army ration system. Like the American employment system was okay if you had a little pull: a case of not what you knew but who you knew. I will say and maintain that if the British soldier received all his dues according to the rules, he had no cause for complaint. Discipline in the Army was very harsh, but a soldier soon began to get used to it and soon fell into line. He was at liberty to cuss at an NCO or officer, providing those parties didn't hear the curses. There's a saying that "you can tame lions in a military prison," and of course it was quite easy to land in one of those institutions. Those who had been there preferred to desert than chance a second term. Most every recruit was likely to kick over the traces, but he was very soon cured after a few hours in the military jug.

Although I had a kind of sneaking regard for the Army, I suddenly came to the conclusion that it was not playing fair, so I decided to desert or as they say in America, "beat it." To do that, however, I knew that I'd be taking a great risk because desertion was considered a cowardly and serious offense, and if I was captured, I'd be punished with at least two years' imprisonment. I also was aware that the responsibility for my apprehension was placed upon the civil police, and those people didn't care to bother much about deserters from the Army. The civil police would usually keep their eyes skinned around the home town of a deserter; otherwise, they never seemed to bother. Maybe they were in sympathy with us. I knew cases where deserters had given themselves up. Anyhow, my mind was made up, so I set about making my plans accordingly. I had to have a little money, so I got in touch with an old married soldier in the canteen and told him my plans, and he said he'd buy my shirts, socks, and boots. He also told me I could get a weekend pass to London. Also, I could obtain an advance of pay if I saw the captain of my company and spun him some hard-luck story.

That night I wrote my mother a letter, telling her to write me a letter, explaining that my brother was very sick and asking if I could get home for a day or two. A couple of days later, armed with her letter, I saw my captain and applied for three days' leave of absence. He scanned my letter and then looked me up and down for a moment as if doubting my letter, asked me a few questions about my brother, and appeared to be satisfied with my answer. He then asked me about money; I told him I had none. Turning to the sergeant, he said, "Make him out a pass and advance him one pound." Then turning to me again, he told me to be back on time or wire for an extension. Getting away from the office, I felt as if I was walking on air. One whole pound. I hadn't seen that amount of money for months.

That night I slept in a real bed in London after feasting in one of the cheap restaurants. I couldn't realize I was free, no reveille or bugle calls in the morning for me. I'd go home and get out of my uniform while the time was good; I had two more days before I'd be reported absent. I arrived home and told my mother that I'd finished with the Army. She was a little bit scared that I'd get into trouble, but I told her not to worry. I got into one of my old suits, borrowed a little money, and was away back in London in no time. After a couple of days tramping around, I got a job as barman in the Strand, one of London's busy thoroughfares. The job had cost me my last five shillings. That establishment was one of a chain of such places situated all over London. They were rather select houses and catered only to the most respectable classes, but I soon found out that I'd quit one Army only to jump right into another one, only a little different in nature. The personnel of these houses were composed of four barmen, one cellarman, a manager, and a woman cook. We sold only the very finest of beer, wines, and liquors. As barman, my duty was to be down in the bar at eight-thirty in the morning. Twenty minutes were allowed for dinner but quite a different dinner to what I'd been used to in the Army, another 20 minutes for tea, and we were expected to be back in the bar on time or get a black look from the manager. We were never allowed to converse with each other or with the customers. When not occupied with serving drinks, we had to stand with arms folded in front and stand there like some statue. We were never allowed to sit down behind the bar. We were allowed out one night every two weeks and one clear day off duty once a month. The pay was very meager. The only good thing about the job was that the firm pensioned its employees after about 30 years of faithful service, but I was a young man, so that pension business didn't seem to appeal to me. So after a month, I decided to quit and once more found myself walking London's streets, looking for work. One day I found myself in Woolwich on the outskirts of London at a large military centre, and before very long, I found myself back in the Army but not in the infantry.

I decided I'd like to have a shot at the horse regiments. In order to do that, I had to change my name and sign myself as Jack Jones from Cardiff, Wales. I then enlisted in the Army Service Corps.

For the second time I'd accepted the King's shilling although not knowing at the time that I'd committed another crime, which besides being a military offense was also a civil offense. If captured, I should be tried and punished by the civil court, and at the expiration of my sentence, I should be duly handed over to the military authorities to face two charges: one for deserting His Majesty's forces, the other for fraudulent enlistment. Therefore, I should be punished twice for committing one offence. For my part, it didn't worry me just because I chose to enlist again, and I couldn't see that it should matter so much. In any case, I couldn't be a soldier in two places at the same time.

The Army Service Corps was known by several names: Commissariet, Supply and Transport, and Ally Sloper's Cavalry. It was our duty to do all the dirty work for the rest of the Army. We were always at their disposal for transportation purposes; if a certain unit was moving from one station to another, we had the job of being responsible for the unit's baggage and that it arrived safely. We supplied daily bread and meat rations, took care of the married families while they were moving, took the sick to hospital, and brought away the discharges, etc. That kind of soldiering was more to my liking. We were always kept busy; day after day, we were out on the streets, getting a change of scene, moving something or somebody about. If a job called for only one wagon or two, we were permitted to go alone, but if there were more than two, there would be an NCO in charge. Unlike the cavalry, we had two horses to take care of, and on returning to barracks, we had plenty to do. The horses had to be thoroughly groomed, watered, fed, and bedded down for the night. Then the harness had to be cleaned and polished, the steel work oiled to prevent rust. The Service Corps was very strict about the horses and harness. Every time, before going out on duty, we had to parade in front of an officer, and he minutely inspected to see everything was spic and span. No excuses were accepted; a dirty link in the harness might mean the loss of three pennies a day to the driver. Once a week, usually on Sundays after church parade, the commanding officer would inspect the stables. All the harnesses were polished and bees-waxed, the steel work burnished like silver, the horses with their heads looking towards the centre of the stable, and each driver standing between his horses' heads. It was all a picturous ceremony. The stables at those times were far cleaner than the barrack rooms.

On joining the corp, I had to go through the ordinary recruit's training, but on account of the corp being more of a working unit, much of the infantry business was cut out, including gymnasium. About a couple of weeks' foot drill on the parade ground was all that was required. One hour a day in the riding school, another couple weeks learning long-rein driving, and I was a full-blown driver, entitled to six pence a day extra pay, which brought my pay up to the large amount of one shilling and nine pence, about fifty cents a day. Out of that I had to find cleaning gear for my uniform, blacking for boots, bees-wax polish and oil for harnesses, etc. I was now eligible for guards and stable picquets furnished every 24 hours. We found one quarter guard at the main gate of the barracks.

Talking about guards, I don't think there was any duty so detestable to a soldier. Guard duties were always monotonous, walking to and fro for 25 yards each way for two hours at a time. If there was something to guard or defend, it might have been a bit more thrilling. What it was all for I failed to see when the regimental police could very well have taken care of that kind of work and more efficiently. For a quarter guard, it took three men and a corporal in charge. The guard room was usually located at the main entrance to the barracks where all soldiers reported on leaving or returning to barracks. The orderly officer of the day would visit the guard twice during a 24-hour duty, once by day and once by night. After his night visit, which was usually between 11 and 12 o'clock, the corporal would go to the gate and bring in some moll and give her a night's shelter in one of the spare cells, leaving us to take care of the guard duties. Occasionally we had the cells all occupied by those butterflies. They carried their own toilet outfits; all they needed was a cup of coffee and permission to wash, and they were all set for another day. We had to chase them off about daybreak. They helped break the monotony of guard duty.

One day I was ordered to report to the master cook for duty. There I was to learn the arts and crafts of Army cooking. In that depot, there were about 1,000 men to cook for, and each cook had about 100 men to cater for. Meal times in the Army had to be ready exactly on time, any hour. Cooked or not, it had to be dished up, an officer standing by while the operation was in progress. The master cook and I became great pals. He was married, and every day he'd send me with some packages to deliver to his wife. He'd wink his eye and say, "My rations, Jack, run them up to the house." Every other day I'd take a wheelbarrow of coal from the cook house to his wife who would give me a bottle of beer. Army life was beginning to get interesting. That was the best job I'd ever struck so far. The best of Army rations was mine by just reaching out my hand, keeping my eyes open and my mouth shut.

After about three months, I was transferred as company cook to a company just returned from South Africa. The company had arrived about half strength and had to be made up to the full complement, about 120 men all told, including officers, NCOs, and men with the usual number of horses and wagons. In about a week, we moved off to take over the Kensington barracks in London W. to do duty in the London district. Everything was going fine for me there; in fact, I wouldn't want to be kicked out of the Army. I was great friends with the Army contractor. I used to sign for 120 pounds of meat and received about 80. I was running the mess book and had about 30 shillings a day to spend on extras which were drawn from the grocery bar. The gifts I received from those two sources were about ten shillings a day, to say nothing about the friends I had in the married quarters who would always see that I never went short of my beer in return for tea, sugar, milk, etc. At the same time, I was always careful to look after my company and see they had plenty. If they went short of a little meat, I could always fill them up with plenty of Army pudding although they would cough up some of that again.

My good luck hadn't come to stay due entirely to my own good nature. The boys would often come to me when they needed a little money a day or so before pay day, and very often I'd take a couple out in London and give them a good time. One night I went out in company with a shoeing smith. He was an old soldier, having been through the Boer War, and was on his last few weeks before getting pensioned off. After several drinks around the Leicester Square district, we decided to go to the Oxford Music Hall. It was a rotten show, so we spent most of the time drinking and talking to the barmaids. By now, we were about full up; we bought a bottle of whiskey each and left with the intention of making for barracks.

We were having some fun with a couple of girls in Tottenham Court Road. Handing the whiskey 'round, my pal started to sing and dropped the bottle of whiskey. We were grabbed by three policemen, taken to the police station, and locked up. There they searched us, took away our tunics, and threw us into a filthy dirty cell occupied by three other drunken men who had done their business on the floor. The following morning we were allowed to wash and were given our breakfast which we paid for and which was brought in from a neighboring restaurant. Neither of us had very little sleep. It was too uncomfortable.

"This is an awful predicament to be in," said Shoey to me. "Wonder what the hell they intend to do to us? Anyhow, we had a damn good night, so I daresay we can take it."

"They had no business to pinch us," I replied. "We weren't too bad. I think it was our being with the girls that did it. Anyhow, it's no use crying over spilt milk."

The officer on duty allowed us to send out for some beer as we were badly in need of an eye opener. About ten o'clock, an ambulance arrived to take us back to barracks where we were confined in the guard room for 24 hours and then marched before the commanding officer. He read out the charge: "Drunk and disorderly in company with prostitutes." Of course, we denied the charge and got away with seven days' CB (confined to barracks). Poor Shoey had to take the blame on account of being an old soldier. The punishment was nothing; it just simply prevented us from going out again for seven days. But worst of all, I'd lost my job and all that went with it. I'd been relieved and returned to duty, which nearly broke my heart and kept me brooding for days after with the notion of deserting again.

Anyhow, to relieve the pain, I was one of a party to be transferred to another company stationed at York, so in due course we left London and arrived at York, an old-fashioned city of gates and bars, old Roman walls and castles, and York Minster, one of the most famous cathedrals in England. York was full of old-fashioned public taverns and pretty women. There I was always in trouble. When I wasn't confined to barracks, I was absent without leave. Once in town, I never could get back to barracks until I was broke. So after a few months, I was on my way to Dublin, Ireland to join the 61st Company stationed in the Royal Barracks.

Dublin. The only city in the world where the streetcars run four abreast on one street. It boasted the largest park in the world and was noted for its fine old buildings. Amongst those were the Bank of Ireland, its castle, and the magnificent Four Courts once badly damaged by Sinn Feiners. It was also the home of the famous Dublin Stout. During my stay in that city, I first saw King Edward VII when he visited Ireland in connection with the Punchestown races. (We were on duty on O'Connell's bridge that spans the River Liffe). On another occasion, we were on duty for the visit of the Prince, later to be King George V. After a few months, my three years with the colours was complete, so I was discharged to do nine years in the Army Reserve and once more returned to civilian life. My reserve pay amounted to six pence a day payable every three months in arrears.

Chapter 3

My Third Enlistment

Well, I found that work was still very hard to obtain. The world hadn't changed very much during the last three years; there were thousands of unemployed in London. I visited my old company in Kensington, only to find most of my comrades had been transferred to the Army Reserve and I supposed, like myself, were hunting for a job. I knocked about from place to place, getting a temporary job here and there. I also applied to my record office for permission to rejoin the colours, but my request was politely refused; I couldn't be permitted to transfer from the Army Reserve to the Army.

Three years of that loafing around was trying my patience, and I had a sneaking regard for the Army life again. After all, there were no dull days in the Army, so one day, finding myself in Norwich, I made the acquaintance of a recruiting sergeant and before many days was signed up to serve seven years in the Norfolk Regiment, an infantry outfit of the line with its training depot in Norfolk. Within three months, my recruits' training was complete, and I was drafted off to the 1st Battalion station at Aldershot, a large military centre where every branch of the British Army was represented. There were quartered the crack guards regiments, lancers, dragoons, royal horse and field artillery, Army Service Corps, medical corps, and all the infantry of the line. We were continually having large field days and manoeuvres. It was whispered 'round at that time that we were likely to be at war with Germany. That was in 1910 with the war another four years away. Evidently someone knew it was coming. While at Aldershot, the King died; my regiment was hurried off to London to take part in the proclamation ceremonies of King George V and then again for the King's funeral. Large crowds turned out to witness those mournful ceremonies. We returned to Aldershot, the bands playing "We Buried the Bugger and Covered Him Up."

At the Aldershot command rifle meeting, I won several money prizes and was chosen as one of a team to sloop for the Young Soldiers' Cup. Every regiment in the Aldershot command was represented by a team of eight men supposed to have under 12 months' service, hence the name of the cup. The men comprising my team were the queerest bunch of "young" soldiers ever seen. Some of them looked as if they had fought in the Crimean War. But we won the cup, and in the final day of the meeting, amidst a lot of pomp and ceremony, we were presented with a beautiful cup, a money prize, and a silver medal for each man. The cup was to repose in the officers' mess for the next 12 months. That night we were invited to the mess to take a drink of champagne from the cup. Believe me, I was really beginning to like the Army.

One morning I was ordered to report to the orderly room, and as that order was rather unusual, I began to wonder what it was all about because the orderly room was attended only by privates who had committed some military offence. But as no escort was provided, that could not be so in my case. Had they found out something about my fraudulent enlistment? I could think of nothing else. Well, if that was the case, I was ready to own up and take what was coming. The evening previous, I'd taken part in a boxing program and was matched with a fellow who had every advantage over me in height, weight, and reach. We fought three three-minute rounds which resulted in a draw, so we had to fight an extra round with a decision going to my opponent. All that I'd already forgotten, with the exception of a few bruises.

I was marched in front of the CO, who was seated at his desk, the adjutant standing by his side. The CO looked at me and smiled. The adjutant then spoke to me about the fine show of spirit in the boxing match and said he thought that the decision should have been given to me. The CO was therefore pleased to present me with two pounds. He had also ordered that I should be promoted to the rank of provisional lance corporal. That was all.

"March out," he said. The sergeant major pinned a stripe on my arm, what he called the first rung in the ladder. "Don't forget," he said, "that stripe represents power, weight, and responsibility. It doesn't carry any pay, but you'll in due course be promoted to the rank of unpaid lance corporal following which you'll become a paid lance corporal on the regular establishment of the regiment."

With that, he dismissed me. Army life was full of surprises. When I expected punishment, I got praised. I entered those boxing contests only for the sake of winning a little extra spending money, and I'd lost the contest, yet I was better off financially than if I'd won. I could already feel the weight of the stripe on my arm; in fact, it was making me walk lopsided by the weight of my head continually looking at it. I began to wonder how long it would stop there as far as responsibility was concerned.

There was plenty. It fell to my lot to be the first out of bed every morning and to see every other man out. I had to see all beds made up on time, rooms cleaned, windows opened, etc. In fact, I was in complete charge of my barracks room and everything it contained as far as general cleanliness was concerned. I was at the beck and call of every Tom, Dick, and Harry. "Can I do this, Corporal? Can I do that, Corporal?" Many a time I told them to go to hell. One thing I didn't like in the Army and that was domestic work: scrubbing floors, cleaning windows, polishing fire stoves, washing dishes, etc. That I considered woman's work. I never could see it in any other light, and very often I closed my eyes to that sort of work; consequently, I was always being reprimanded for neglect. No, I never could make a barracks room soldier, but outside on the parade ground, I was quite at home. That was what I enlisted for.

As a lance corporal, my duties were numerous and varied. I had to take my turn as NCO in charge of the quarter guards' canteen duty, orderly corporal in charge of fatigue parties, etc. I was immune from punishment by the captain of my company. Any case involving me could be disposed of only by the commanding officer or court-martial. That was the advantage of being an NCO. Never a day passed without prisoners having to be punished for some minor offense, silly trivial affairs. Such was military discipline.

Towards the latter part of 1910, a draft of 200 men including me was to leave England to join the 2nd Battalion, Norfolk Regiment, stationed at Gibraltar and which was under orders to proceed to India. We were all sent on one-month furloughs, including a few waiting men as there were always a few desertions when a draft was going abroad. We were all due back two days before sailing, to be fitted out with sun helmets and foreign service dress: one suit of drill khaki and one pair of shorts per man. The morning arrived for our departure, and headed by two military bands, we marched to Aldershot Station to the tune of "The Girl I Left Behind Me." We pulled out of the station to the strains of "Auld Lang Syne." There was many a man in that draft who was never to see old England again. All in the life of a soldier. We embarked on a transport at Southampton, sailed the same night for Plymouth, picked up a regiment going to South Africa, and proceeded on our way to Gibraltar, where we were met by the regimental band and marched to barracks. There we were to remain a month before proceeding to India.

Except for the rock itself, there was nothing very attractive about Gibraltar. Nothing in particular grew on the rock although there were a few monkeys that had been there for years. It was a large fortress, had a large number of concealed guns mounted in the numerous caves, and was supposed to have enough preserved rations to withstand a siege for years if necessary. At the north end was an old Moorish castle, and Europa Point at the southern end commanded a view to the entrance of the Mediterranean Sea. It was also a large naval base capable of docking Britain's largest battleships. Large numbers of Spaniards who came over from Spain every day were employed in the dockyards. They had to be off the rock each day by sunset or they had to remain all night because at sunset the gates which commanded the neutral zone were locked.

The locking of those gates was quite a ceremonial military pageant. Headed by the band and drums in full military review order, a company of soldiers marched with fixed bayonets guarding a man who carried the keys. Upon arrival at the gates, the buglers sounded the tattoo; the gates were then locked, to be opened again at sunrise the following morning. The neutral zone was only a few hundred yards, a piece of ground used as a football field by British soldiers.

There was also a licensed red-light district which did a thriving business when the fleet was in port. A large naval canteen catered for both Army and Navy. It had one main business street occupied by Moors and Spaniards where money was exchanged. Gibraltar was very valuable to the British government in that it commanded all shipping entering and leaving the Mediterranean Sea, but it was a very monotonous place from a soldier's point of view. Thank goodness we had only a month to remain there.

The day arrived to embark for India. We were relieved by a regiment from England and embarked on the ship which brought the regiment out: the hired transport *Plassy*, a one-funnel ship which had been converted into a troopship belonging to the P and O Line and used for passenger service between London and Australia.

To the strains of "Auld Lang Syne," the rock gradually faded behind us as we steamed out to sea. Life aboard a trooper was carried out as near as possible very much the same as in barracks. We got the same old bugle calls from reveille to lights out. Beer was issued twice a day; the food was good, provided by the ship's company. The recreation was left to ourselves to provide. There were all kinds of stores where we could purchase cigarettes, candy, etc. (Smoking was strictly prohibited after lights out.)

We dropped a few details at Malta and then stopped again at Port Said to coal the ship. There a few of the senior officers were allowed ashore. We had to be content looking over the ship's side and amusing ourselves throwing pennies into the sea for the natives to dive for, causing us lots of fun.

Proceeding through the Suez Canal and the Red Sea, we dropped a few more details at Aden, a barren-looking possession at the extreme end of the Red Sea. The soldiers who were quartered there were relieved every 12 months on account of the climatic conditions which prevailed there. It was extremely hot and uncomfortable, and those living there had to depend on the rains for water stored in large tanks made for that purpose. Talk to any soldier about Aden, and he'd tell you, "It's a bad egg." One more week at sea, and we sighted the coast of India. It was the first time we young soldiers had been so far from home, and feeling a bit cramped, we were all glad the voyage was over. The chaplain called a church service and gave thanks for the safe passage of all concerned. We were then paid out in English gold; we all had about three weeks' pay coming, and of course we could use it if we got out in Bombay.

We dropped anchor some distance from the docks, and money changers came aboard and changed our English sovereigns for India rupees at the rate of 15 to the pound. Those money changers were big fat Parsees and wore big shiny black tin hats, making them easily distinguished from the ordinary natives. The Parsees ran most of the big business concerns in India. I never saw a poor one. They were supposed to be some of the remnants chased out of Persia years ago. We could always see them as they worshiped the sun going down in the west.

We were taken off the ship and run ashore in big lighters to a covered-in shed with railroad tracks running alongside. After a meal of tea and sandwiches, we entrained for Belgaum, a cantonment some miles south of Poona. It was twilight, and we could see very little of Bombay as the train passed through that city. It was very hot and uncomfortable although all the windows were open. At Poona we left the GIP tracks for the BSMR small gauge which was to take us on the last stage of our journey and which took a few hours because all our baggage had to be manhandled and carried some distance in a most distressing heat. The CO was very pleased with the way we carried out the work and ordered extra tea to be served. Troop trains moved very slowly in India, but eventually we arrived at Belgaum where more tea and sandwiches awaited us. No pleasure riding troop trains in India. If a soldier slept at all, it must be done sitting up; no sleeping accommodation was provided for. After the sweating of getting the baggage loaded into bullocks carts, we marched about a mile to barracks.

India

It took us about a week to get used to our surroundings and settle down. We were the only British regiment with the exception of a battery of field artillery; the other three regiments were native infantry whom we were never allowed to mix with under no circumstances. The combined outfit made up the Belgaum brigade and part of the 6th Poona division. The GOC paid us a visit, praised us up on our smart general appearance, and told us that plenty of hard work and exercise was essential to health and happiness in India.

The first thing that appealed to a soldier in India was the large number of natives who were employed in barracks. The barracks were composed of large well-ventilated bungalows of stone. From a distance, some of them might be mistaken for a stone or marble palace, quite a different contrast to what we had been used to in England. Everything was done for the welfare, health, and comfort of the soldier. Two hundred pounds was supposed to be the value of the life of a private in the Indian Army. A soldier in India was everything the name implied in England; he was more or less a domesticated servant. The natives who were employed belonged to the quartermaster's staff. There were the native cooks supervised by a European, tailors, barbers, sweepers, water carriers, cleaners who looked after the latrines. The married women were supplied with native servants. Then there were native policemen who took care of that army of native workers. Soldiers were supplied with a native servant who cleaned his buttons and shoes, made up his bed, and made it down; in fact, he did everything with the exception of cleaning a soldier's equipment and rifle. Those two things a native was never allowed to touch, and he knew it.

Every morning between three and five the barber came and shaved every soldier in bed, so when a soldier rose, all he had to do was to wash and put on his uniform to be spic and span, all ready for parade. Thursdays and Saturdays were holidays, and a soldier was permitted to go and do as he pleased. The country surrounding Belgaum was all jungle and infested with snakes, so it wasn't safe to go about unless armed with a big stick. Putties were always worn as a precaution against snakebite. There were 20,000 natives who died annually from snakebite. But unlike us, the native, when bitten, refused to take treatment and was prepared to die, which he often did.

Time often dragged on account of the day's duties being through about ten o'clock and because of the terrific heat outside the bungalows. There were the recreation rooms, a well-stocked library where billiards and other games were indulged in, and of course the beer canteen which was open for one hour at midday and from six to nine-thirty at night and which sold good beer imported from Scotland.

There were also good attractive positions offered to soldiers who could qualify. A soldier who held a 2nd-class Army certificate could, if he so desired, be trained as an engine driver at one of the large railway depots, and at the completion of his training, he was permitted to work at his job although he was still a soldier doing civilian work and getting paid for both jobs. He might then at the expiration of his Army service take his discharge and remain in India with a good job. Strange to say, very few took advantage of that offer. Then there was a course in telegraphy at the post office which also offered the same advantage. A soldier might also, on completing his colour service, enter the Indian Civil Police Department, also a good-paying position, saying nothing about the baksheesh attached to the job. But as a rule, a soldier on completion of his time turned his nose west to England; somehow India didn't appeal to an ex-soldier.

In India as England, a soldier had a tough job holding onto his money which he had to spend for extra food. The Army rations in India were plentiful in quantity but not quality; the meat which was of course killed fresh daily was too tough for consumption even after hours of stewing. The meat was then thrown to the dogs or to the kite hawks which were always around the barracks. Butter was made from buffalo milk and didn't have a very pleasing taste. The tea which was issued was of a very inferior nature, compared to that which could be purchased in the coffee shop. The consequence was that a soldier would never tackle his Army rations as long as he had the price of a meal in his pocket; the best part of a soldier's pay went to the regimental coffee shops or to the YMCA and soldiers' homes which catered special dishes for a very moderate charge. Good food in India was plentiful and cheap, especially eggs, chicken, duck, fish, etc., and for eight annas (about 15 cents), a good chicken dinner could always be obtained. There was what's known as the credit system and was worked by the coffee shop and canteen contractor, usually a Parsee merchant. He had little printed tickets valued at one rupee which might be obtained on the signature of the soldier and could be exchanged at the regiment's institutes for eatables, cigarettes, beer, etc. The consequence was that on pay day the soldiers had nothing coming and was always more or less in debt, to the advantage of the contractor.

A soldier on leave in India was permitted to travel on the railways at half the usual fare, and if he was wise and made friends with the train staff, he could travel free; a bottle of whiskey worked wonders. A good soldier was permitted 90 days leave every year if he wished but wasn't allowed to leave India.

Those long leaves were many often times shooting parties. About half a dozen men would get together to make up a party, and off they'd go into the jungle areas which abounded all over India. There was always plenty of sport in shooting game: pea fowl and cheetah. Tigers and lions we left to the more experienced big-game hunters. Very little money was needed for these parties as we depended on what we killed for provisions. Native villages were barred for us, and all water had to be boiled before drinking. On those expeditions, we carried rifles and guns for buckshot. Although those parties were very enjoyable, we were glad to get back long before the expiration of the leave.

Those leaves weren't restricted to shooting parties; some soldiers went to the large cities such as Bombay, Calcutta, Bangalore, etc. where there was always good accommodation either in barracks or soldiers' homes, YMCA, etc. Some would visit other cantonments. I spent one leave at Secunderabad in the Nizam's dominion in central India. The native ruler went by the name of His Exalted Highness, the Nizam of Hyderabad. He was the only ruler in India who was permitted to own his own army. He maintained an army of infantry, cavalry, and artillery and was entitled to a salute of 21 guns. He was reputed to be very wealthy and was the owner of his own private railways. He had several wives who went around in a large fleet of up-to-date motor cars. He collected taxes from his millions of toddy trees which abounded his estates. Those toddy trees were tapped by the natives who collected the toddy and barreled it up to be sent to the bazaars and cities. The toddy was of a milky colour and if drank in large quantities produced an effect similar to our beer. It was very refreshing when taken direct from the tree. Many a morning after a big night in the canteen, we would get up early and climb one of those trees for a drink of toddy although we had to strain the large black ants with our teeth. Sometimes the native owners would come along and for a few pice would supply us with all we needed. Toddy drinking was strictly against the military rules.

Back in Belgaum, it would be time to start the training season which would occupy our time for a couple of months. It would start with company training and finish up with divisional manoeuvres on a grand scale, taking the form of two opposing forces, both native and British, partaking in these operations and carried out strictly according to active service conditions.

There were church services every Sunday morning which was the occasion for a very impressive ceremony. Since the Indian mutiny broke out while most of the troops were at church—the natives raided the barracks and took all they could lay their hands on, including rifles, equipment, etc.—the soldiers marched to church fully armed with fixed bayonets; rifles were locked and the bolts removed, and there was always a plentiful supply of ammunition stored in the barracks rooms, ready for any emergency which might arise. The windows and doors were never closed except during the monsoon or rainy season. There was always a soldier on duty in every bungalow night and day, a soldier whose duty it was to report any unusual occurrence. There were of course the ordinary guard duties to perform, such as quarter guard, magazine guard, etc. (Magazine guards were most always furnished by a British unit.)

The rainy season which lasted from middle of June to middle of September was the main supply of water used in India. Much of the water was collected in large wells which abounded the country. During those rains, charcoal was burnt in the bungalows to help keep the dampness out, but during monsoon season everything turned mildew. By the time the monsoon weather was due to appear, water supplies ran low, and the rainy season's failure to arrive would cause disease, famine, and hardship on the millions of natives.

The Army schools in India were for the education of the children belonging to the married establishment of the regiment, which was about five percent. The strength of a British regiment numbered about 1,000 men, including all ranks. The schools were used in the evening for soldiers' classes. For a soldier to receive first-class pay, he has to be in possession of a third-class certificate; with a second-class, he might obtain promotion up to the rank of sergeant. All ranks above sergeant were required to hold first-class certificates which entitled them to be addressed as "Sir" on being approached by an inferior rank. Commissions might be granted under certain rules and regulations.

There were still quite a large number of old forts in India which were occupied by troops; there was one at Belgaum situated about three miles from barracks. It was occupied by one company, and on account of its unhealthy nature was relieved every month by a fresh company of men. Large doses of quinine were issued two or three times a week on account of malaria. The fort occupied a space about a half mile square and was infested with snakes and mosquitoes.

What the buildings contained was a military secret, but they were generally believed to contain personnel rations and ammunition. It was a weird, uncanny place, especially at nighttime. It contained an old Indian temple with a big stone image which had half a dozen arms and legs and a head looking like a cross between an elephant and pig. Every night between midnight and two o'clock, an uncanny noise which sounded like the rattling of heavy chains accompanied by the bawling of a cow would break the stillness of the night. Yet there were no animals either in or outside the fort which had only one entrance. That gate was always locked and could only be entered by persons giving the password.

Early in November 1911, the regiment proceeded to Bombay to take part in the forthcoming ceremonies of receiving the King, who was on his way out from England to visit India in connection with being crowned Emperor, and elaborate arrangements were made to greet him. That was the first time in history that any living person had beheld his ruler enthroned at Durban in the Indian Empire, and during that occasion, the capitol was moved from Calcutta to Delhi.

The regiment arrived in Bombay about a week before the King was due to arrive, and we were quartered in the old mint facing the harbour. Every day we paraded, headed by the regimental band, and marched with fixed bayonets 'round the city. On the day the King arrived off Bombay, he was greeted with the usual salute of guns from the shore batteries, a salute which was returned by his escort of warships. He came ashore at the Apollo Bunder and inspected the guard of honour of selected men, most of them wearing the South Africa medals. He stopped occasionally to chat to some old soldiers. The main body of the regiment was on line duty, keeping the crowds in order. With the usual military ceremony, the King and Queen drove through the streets of Bombay in an open carriage and were cheerfully greeted everywhere by his native subjects who turned out in the thousands to see their great white chief. For days after, Bombay was one great city of bunting and gala parties; all the ships in harbour and those standing out to sea were all dressed up and at night were illuminated with small coloured electric lights and with a large searchlight display, making a beautiful reflection on the water. Leave was granted to the fleet, and Bombay was flooded with soldiers and sailors, the likes of which had never been seen before or since. We remained in Bombay until after the King's departure and then returned to our station in Belgaum.

The King must have been very pleased with his visit because the day he sailed from India, he left orders that all ranks which had taken part in his Durban celebrations were to receive half a month pay according to rank as a gratuity. Some of the boys said that he must have made the order while he was having just one more whiskey and soda and forgot to cancel the order the next morning. Anyhow, we received the money, and that night everybody was singing "God Save the King" as loud as his lungs would allow. The bar, too, seemed to be a little extra crowded that night, as some of us woke up in the guard room next morning facing a charge of being drunk—a minor affair if not accompanied by more serious offenses.

Venereal Diseases

For a long time the spread of venereal disease amongst British troops in India was causing the authorities some anxiety. On entering India, a young soldier was issued a little pamphlet written in simple language, warning against contracting diseases from native women. The disease had been the means of cutting short many a promising young soldier's career. Contracting a venereal disease was a punishable offense. Soldiers who contracted the disease would, partly through ignorance, try to treat themselves and suffer in silence. From the moment he contracted the disease, his efficiency pay automatically ceased, he was treated for several weeks in hospital, and was eventually sent home to England, broken in health and spirit to be a burden amongst his friends.

So the authorities were determined to find the source of the disease and stamp it out. They found out that soldiers would go out and pick up the low-caste women who could be found on the country roads; usually those women would pretend to be gathering twigs and encourage the soldiers into the jungle with them. The "sand rats," as we called them, were rounded up and disposed of but with very poor results. At last a plan was put into effect which was supposed to have originated from the viceroy's wife. And so it came about that a section of the bazaar where British soldiers were quartered was set apart for the convenience of soldiers wishing to meet their "girlfriends." Those places became known to the soldiers as "the bull ring." The rings were well stocked with pretty, dusky damsels ranging in age from about 17 upwards. The girls came under the supervision of the medical authorities and were subject to weekly inspections, and if by any chance a soldier became infected from one of those girls, he was taken to the bull ring and the girl was made a prisoner and sent to hospital. At the entrance to the bull rings, there was a little spot where a soldier had to wash himself both on entering and leaving. That method seemed to have had a great effect in containing the disease.

Marriage for a private was out of the question. White women were very seldom seen outside of the married quarters of the regiment and the homes of government officials. It sometimes happened that a soldier would marry some Eurasian girl; most were of a darker complexion than the ordinary native. The only difference was that the Eurasian was the daughter of a native woman and a European father or vice versa. Eurasian girls were fairly well educated and could speak both English and Industani, but such a union was a great mistake and was never encouraged as it was sure to end in complete disaster. I remember on one occasion when I was on a visit to Bangalore, a young soldier had got involved with a Eurasian family. He started off by getting acquainted with the old man who was working in the barracks; the man was an old soldier on pension and had married a Eurasian woman and reared a large family. He had two very pretty daughters, but their skin was as black as coal, and it was the ambition of those girls to mate up with a white man if possible. Well, that young man got so intimate with the family that eventually he found himself in trouble with one of the girls. Although he didn't wish to marry her, the family raised so much hell that he finally married the girl. His married life appeared to be quite happy until his regiment received orders to return to England. Then the trouble started. He found it would be impossible for him to take that black woman to England with him, so a few days before the regiment was due to sail, he was found dead with his throat cut from ear to ear. Rather than face the music, he had preferred death. As Rudyard Kipling said, "East Is East, West Is West, and never the twain shall meet." That no doubt was probably true and part of the game in the life of a soldier.

War

In 1914 we'd been stationed at Belgaum three years, and we knew the names of every hill, knoll, nullah, ravine, and every inch of the country in that district for miles around and were under orders to proceed to Jubbalpore for an exchange of stations. We were all pleased at that news, as it was beginning to get rather dull in that jungle home. Then in August the news came over the wires that we were at war with Germany which at once put a stop to all troop movements in India, and we received orders to "stand by." Such news caused no little excitement, and we wondered what part we were going to play in the great struggle. The news flashes which reached us daily didn't appear to be very cheerful, especially when we heard that the German armies had overrun Belgium and were already upon French soil with Paris as their objective. Although we were already hardened to active service conditions and considered one of the best fighting units then in India, we buckled to and started training with more rigor than ever. Every day we were out in the boiling heat, practicing all kinds of war stunts which we were already acquainted with and could accomplish with our eyes shut. Long night marches were endured, with our leaving barracks at sunset and finishing up about sunrise with a mimic attack on some imaginary enemy. Imaginary fighting was all right, of course, but we soon wearied of such stuff. What we needed and were looking for was the real game.

Even the regimental band was continually playing patriotic airs which helped to stir us up a little more. The days dragged by and turned into weeks; the suspense of waiting was getting unbearable. Still we received no orders. What was wrong with our regiment? Once in a while a rumour would go around that we were going, going, going. Yes, we were going crazy. Here was one of the finest regiments which ever marched the burning plains of India, every mother's son as hard as the holes of hell, all itching to get off to the war. Had the Army Council forgotten about our existence? Surely not. India at that time was enjoying one of its quiet spells, so there was no earthly reason why we shouldn't be alongside of our pals on the Western Front. We received the news about the capture of Liege and the Battle of the Marne. We began to give up hopes of ever getting in the war; at that time, most of us expected the war to be over in a few weeks.

One day we received orders to dispose of our pets. Most every soldier owned a pet of some kind: dogs, cats, monkeys, parrots, pigeons, etc. There were almost as many dogs as there were men in the regiment. Dogs were shot and buried, most of the pigeons were killed and eaten, monkeys and parrots were sold or given away, the cats were left to take care of themselves. Those orders seemed to indicate that we were making a move, but no, another couple of weeks slipped by.

Our being in a kind of disheartened mood, some of the boys started to drown their sorrows in drink. Needless to say, those boys from Norfolk could drink; I think they must have been weaned on beer. Those who had managed to save a few rupees drew their savings out, and the beer canteen was doing a roaring business. Picture the drunken mob of soldiers in the canteen: some were singing songs that were popular at that time, such as the "Robert E. Lee" and "Alexander's Ragtime Band," etc.; others were slouching at the tables, arguing about the war and asking why they weren't in it. Some were so full up that they were kidding that they had already been to the war and just come back, by imitating a disabled soldier with a leg or arm gone. The older soldiers were sitting in a corner by themselves, saying nothing but enjoying every moment of the show. They were watching the young bloods and probably wondering how they would shape up when they found themselves up against a wall of bayonets. Those old soldiers had had some, their memory still young, having fought in the South Africa [Boer] War of 1899–1902. We didn't hear them saying much about wanting to go to war.

The evening usually finished up outside the canteen in a free and easy fight for all, but what they were fighting about was hard to explain. A few would land in the guard room and remain there for 48 hours to sober up. Some had to be punished. That sort of behaviour went on night after night and got so serious that the CO decided to close the canteen and limit open hours to two a day. This order proved to be an unfortunate one, for to cut Tommies' beer off meant they immediately set about finding it elsewhere, which they did through the help of the natives in the bazaar. But instead of getting beer, soldiers were getting supplied with whiskey and native arrack both of which were forbidden to British soldiers. The bazaar merchants were under a severe penalty if caught supplying soldiers with intoxicating drinks of any kind. Of course, the merchants would never sell directly to a soldier, but a little baksheesh to a wandering native worked miracles, and the trick was done. Needless to say, it didn't take the authorities very long to find out what was going on, so the next thing that happened was the bazaars were placed "out of bounds," and of course any soldier disobeying that order was severely punished. The bazaars were frequently placed out of bounds during the course of a year for various reasons, such as a cholera scare, dog rabies, or some other disease; on those occasions, soldiers were confined to their own quarters. Although the taps were now turned off officially, whiskey was mysteriously appearing from some source, so it was decided to open the canteen again. Most of those young Norfolk men were the descendents of fighting families, fathers and grandfathers having been in the service before them and having fought in the Crimean War of 1854–1856 and the Sudan-Egyptian campaigns with General Gordon. It didn't seem to cheer them up on hearing the news that a battery of artillery had left Bangalore and that a cavalry regiment had left Secunderbad for the war zone; however, their turn did come, and as you'll see later, they had plenty of it.

It was discovered that there were a few German people residing in Belgaum, and in due course, they were rounded up and interred only as a precautionary measure although no doubt they were harmless, having lived in India for years. One of those gentlemen whom we'll call Fritz was in business. He lived in a large bungalow, part of which he turned into a restaurant and pool room and did quite a large volume of business amongst the troops. His food and drinks were the very best obtainable this side of Bombay, and his beer which he was not supposed to sell but was for his own consumption only had the strength of the Rock of Gibraltar. He also played the Good Samaritan to his advantage when being approached for a small loan on the simple promise to repay with "a little interest" as Fritz called it. What money wasn't spent in barracks was scooped in by Fritz. He had all kinds of attractions to amuse the troops, including two fine strapping daughters of a marriageable age who were as scarce as flies were plentiful in an outlandish place like Belgaum. Needless to say, those girls became great favourites of the troops. Those girls also had their special favourites, but occasionally they'd transfer their affections so that everyone got a peek. It came as a great surprise when they were interred, not so much on account of the old man, but the girls, oh dear, the girls were also interred. The only amusement of the regiment was interrupted; that was hell, and for the time being it was the chief topic for conversation. Poor old Fritz was hit pretty hard because he was thus deprived from making his livelihood. We all felt sorry for him because he was a pretty good sort to us lonely soldiers; he was more generous than otherwise and always gave us good value for our money.

It was about the middle of October when the regiment received orders to be prepared to move at 24 hours' notice. (It had been noticed that the station yard was full of passenger cars which was rather unusual.) So it had come at last, and that news caused more noise than two express trains hitting head on, traveling hundreds of miles an hour. What for months we had been waiting for had come. What was the matter? Had everybody been killed or what? Did they really need us? At first, we thought it was a joke but oh no; it was only too true, only a matter of hours. Cheerful, why, everyone was cheerful. The boozing suddenly ceased, and the boys went about their duties more seriously, waiting for the next bomb to burst. It did burst the next day in the form of a medical examination for every man going on active service. Every man's medical history sheet was examined. The parade of "patients" lasted all day, and that night the names of the men who were going was posted on the company's notice board. Few, however, were requested; some men had some little defect and were given the option of going or staying behind. Others who had contracted certain venereal diseases whilst in India were rejected. That rejection nearly broke those men's hearts. Nothing hurt a soldier more than to see his regiment going away and leaving him behind whether it be going to war or elsewhere.

All our spare equipment was packed and put into storage, including bedding, barrack room cleaning utensils, etc. All we possessed now was our fighting order equipment, comprising rifle, ammunition, bayonet, and a blanket. All other miscellaneous stuff which always accumulates was disposed of in the ordinary military fashion. Every man was given an active service pay book which included a printed page in the form of a will which he had to sign with the name and address of the person who was to benefit in case of his death. We then each received our metal identification disk, bearing our rank, regimental number, name of regiment, and name of the owner. We were ordered to place these disks around our necks by the string attached and told not to remove them until the war was over.

Then came news that the Germans had captured Antwerp which made us more anxious to get going before they captured London. We no doubt imagined we could stop them once we got there. All we thought about was France and the Western Front, giving little thought to any other part of the war zone. We were all sure we were going to France, but would we?

The next day we said farewell to the regimental colours, a kind of solemn ceremony. During the old wars, the colours always accompanied the regiment into battle, but for some reason that didn't happen any more. During normal times the colours were housed in the officers' mess, but in the "new war," they were placed for safekeeping with some responsible official of the town or city. In the latter case, they were placed in the city's treasury for safekeeping until such time as the regiment should return and claim them. On that most important occasion of farewell, a general parade of the regiment was ordered. Every available man had to attend with the exception of men on guard and other special duties. The whole regiment was formed up in quarter column formation of double companies on the general parade ground. The colour party arrived carrying the colours unfurled, on which in gold letters were inscribed the names of the various battles which the regiment had already taken part in, dating some hundreds of years back. Headed by the regimental band, we marched off in columns of four, over 1,000 strong, to the city treasury where the colours were to repose in safe custody indefinitely.

Arriving at the treasury, the regiment was lined up two deep on either side of the road and ordered to "present arms." The colours were then marched through the whole length of the regiment while the band played the regimental march, "Rule Britannia." Finally, the colours disappeared into the treasury. Many of us had said farewell to the colours for the last time. There was a vast crowd of native spectators watching the ceremony, no doubt wondering what it was all about. The battalion then reformed and marched back to barracks to the tune of "The Girl I Left Behind Me."

That night a little after midnight we were quietly aroused from our slumber and marched by companies to the railway station, and in the early hours of the morning before the native population was awake, the 2nd Battalion Norfolk Regiment steamed out of Belgaum en route to the Great War. France, yes, we were certain we were going to France. But the only part of France that a few of the lucky ones saw was some five years later when we crossed that country on the way home to Merrie England. Anyhow, the Norfolk "dumplins" were at last in the height of their glory; nothing else mattered. The troop trains operated by the Maratta and Southern India Railway Company were designed for the conveyance of natives and were infested with bed bugs. Vermin attacked us in the millions, keeping us busy until we left them at Poona, where we transferred to the Great Indian Peninsular Lines for the trip to Bombay where we arrived all in the best of health and spirits after a rather uncomfortable journey in the bug-eaten trains. We tumbled out of the train at the docks, lined up into companies, stacked our rifles, and were permitted to take things easy for a while.

It was there in that great Bombay dockyard that we could see that there really was a war going on. The docks were full of great ocean-going ships. There were all kinds of officers, both Indian and European, flying about everywhere in their strange-looking uniforms: British staff officers wearing red tabs on their collars, others with white bands on their arms with the word "embarkation." Indian soldiers and native police were on duty guarding all kinds of war material, most of the ships were loading up war stores, ships' officers on the bridge were throwing out orders, cussing and swearing most of the time at some little thing which had gone wrong. Most moments they were bellowing something through a large megaphone. Quartermasters were cursing the native crews, and serangs were rushing and pushing the sailors along with the workers speaking in their native language which most of us didn't understand. But activity there certainly was and plenty of it. Every hour brought trainloads of troops with large guns, cases of ammunition, preserved rations, horses and mules with small mountain guns on their backs. All that war material was quickly transferred to the ships which were continually being pulled out to sea by large tugs. It was a great sight and something new to us. Never before had we seen so many guns and machines for the destruction of mankind.

Owing to some alterations being made in the ship we were to board, we were delayed; she was being converted from a cargo into a troop ship and was still in the hands of the carpenters when we arrived at the docks.

It must have been November 3rd because the news had just come through that Turkey had joined the war on the side of Germany. That news of course gave us plenty to talk about. We didn't want to go to Turkey. We preferred to have turkey on a plate covered with some spuds and green peas. The bugle sounded the "fall in," and within a few seconds, every man was in his place. Then the bugle sounded the pay call. "Get your pay books ready and line up to receive your pay." The next order was "leave," which was met with a rousing cheer because we were all pretty well broke although there was nothing to buy on the docks except a bottle of pop and a beer.

Every man received 30 rupees, about 10 dollars American money. On an ordinary pay day, we never received above five or six rupees, so we felt like little millionaires with so much money all in silver coin. We would have liked to go and have a look around Bombay, but we'd received strict orders not to leave the docks which was practically impossible to do anyway as all the gates were patrolled by military police and those gates were the only means of exit, the docks bounded by walls about 16 feet high with spiked railings mounted on top. Most of the boys had launched in little groups playing cards although gambling was strictly prohibited in the Army. A couple of pals, Jack and Peter, and I went on a tour of the docks and were invited aboard one of the ships and had a good meal and a few drinks. Our newly found friends sent us off loaded with tattoos and cigarettes, and feeling slightly acclimated, we began looking around for some more booze.

"I dunno what the hell they wanted to keep us tied up in this damn dockyard for," said Jack.

"Nor me," said Peter. "This pocketful of rupees is kind of making me feel overbalanced."

Peter stopped a native coolie: "Here boy, you want baksheesh, you go bazaar and get me bottle of whiskey."

"English may mellum, sahib, may mellum," said the native.

Then Peter introduced his Industani: "Foom Industani jaunter."

"Acha, sahib, Industanibojanntes," replied the native. "Here puch-roo doo rahee bazaar jaunter. Foom puch-roo ach houie puggle paw-nee juldec karroo. Fich sahib."

And off went the boy with Peter's two rupees. He returned in about half an hour with two bottles of beer and one rupee.

"Well, did you ever see such a black son of a bitch; come here, you dumb black guard. You pay one rupee for two bottles of beer?" said Peter.

"Me ney mellum English jahile."

"Give him a note," said Jack back, so Peter wrote, "Please supply bearer with one bottle of Scotch whiskey," which the boy brought back with half rupee change, saying "Salaam, sahib. Fich hai, sahib."

Peter told him to keep the change which was as much as the poor devil could have earned in a week at his ordinary labour. By the time the bottle of whiskey was consumed, Jack and Peter thought it was time to have a look around Bombay. So leaving them in that mood, I gave no more thought to Jack and Peter, knowing that it was impossible for them to leave the dockyard.

"Come on, you damn son of a Norfolk farmer; let's go and see something," said Peter. "This 'ere war will all be over before we get there an' this is the first war and the last war I was ever in, and I don't want it ta finish too quickly 'cos I want ta handle a lot more of these thirty rupee stunts. Talk about the Army: 'Come on boys, join the Army; it's a damn good Army.'"

"For chrissake, what the hell is the matter with you?" said Jack. "You're talking about a good Army."

"It's the first time I heard you say that; you said last week that this Army was no damn good. Yes you did, so don't deny it, the way yer throwing yerself about 'cause you got a few marbles in yer pocket. Anybody would think you was some unpaid adjunct or something. I moves to crack the Army up and to hell with the Army," said Peter. "Come on, and let's forget we're in the blooming Army for a few hours. Anyhow, we got till tomorrow morning before we join the Army again, so let's go and see if we can drop a few bombs on Bombay."

With that, my two pals wandered off. I don't suppose either knew where they were going.

I made my way back to where the regiment was to find the rest of the boys having a real time. A military band was playing popular songs, and soldiers were dancing Irish jigs and Scottish reels. A canteen had opened up and was selling lots of beer. That was our last night in Bombay. The next day we were leaving.

At roll call the next morning, there was as usual a few absentees, and amongst them were my two pals, Jack and Peter. I thought that perhaps they were coiled up somewhere in the docks, the weather being such that a drunken soldier would sleep anywhere. Search parties were sent out and around the docks, had they, in their state, fallen into the waters. I didn't think so although it was quite possible in that strange place. I'd seen that pair drunk many times, and neither of them had the sense of a mule when in that state.

About nine o'clock the orderly sergeant beckoned to me and said, "Read that," as he handed me a paper:

To OC 2nd Norfolk Regiment
Bombay Dock 6 November 1914

Sir:
No. 8334 Pte J. Gibson and No. 8459 Pte P. Harris, soldiers of the 2nd Norfolk Regiment, were apprehended last night about 12 o'clock midnight and are now detained here. Please send escort.

Ch. Hudson, Commandant MP, Detention Barracks

So they had got out after all.

"I wondered what the devil those two fellows had been up to," said the sergeant to me. "A couple of good fellows when they're not full up with booze. Take two men and bring them back here. Go as quickly as you can. Better hire a gharry because we never know the moment when we have to go aboard."

With my escort, I arrived at the detention barracks and presented myself to the commandant, signed a document, and soon had Jack and Peter in my custody.

"Here," said the commandant and handed me a large, thick envelope. "That is the documentary evidence. Take care of it because we have no duplicates."

I saluted him, said "Very good, Sir" and away we marched.

That pair surely looked a sorrowful sight. If they had been pulled through the barrel of a gun (were that possible), they couldn't have looked any worse. Peter had lost his helmet, had two lovely black eyes, and his nose looked as if it had been hit with a hammer; his uniform was unsightly, covered with blood and was minus one of its buttons. Jack wasn't much better. I couldn't help laughing to myself. It was impossible to march them through the streets; people would think it was a circus, so the five of us got into a gharry.

"Got a cigarette, Corporal?" said Jack. "I've lost mine and all my money, too. I'm clean stoney broke, and only yesterday I had 30 rupees.

Give me a smoke, Corporal, and you might pull up at some place and let me treat you to a bottle of beer. I'm nearly dead for the want of a drink."

I could see they were both in a bad way, so I told the gharry-wallah to take us to the nearest place although I was taking a chance, knew it was against the rules, and would go pretty bad with me if we were caught.

After refreshing themselves with a beer and some cheese, they appeared a little more cheerful. "That's better," said Peter. "Oh boy. I'll say I was thirsty. I believe I could have drank a bucket of sea water. Thanks, Corporal. I believe you saved my life."

"What excuses have you got for getting yourselves into this hell of a mess? I'm telling you that it's going to be just too bad for the pair of you; you look more like as if you had just returned from the war instead of just going."

"You can blame it all on this bloody fool here," said Jack. "He takes me out, gets me drunk, gets me all messed up in a fight with some sailors, and then gets me landed in jail. Then he says he's my pal."

"A bloody good pal you are! Why, you ain't got the guts you was born with. That's right, that's right, to try to put it all onto my shoulders," yelled Peter.

"You bloody yokel, for chrissake, don't you ever come out with me again, some pal you are. What do you think we'll get for this, Corporal? Do you think it's a serious affair?" said Jack.

"It's a serious case, all right, and it's quite possible you may wind up by finding yourselves in front of a firing squad. Do you realize that you're on active service now, and absentees and deserters are punished by death? Both of these crimes can be brought against you, but it also depends upon the evidence in the envelope."

"You don't mean to say that they can shoot us?" said Peter, his gills turning a little pale.

"Oh, yes," said I. "They don't fool with the likes of you on active service; you're what they term one of the King's bad bargains."

"Don't you think you could say something for us, Corporal, to make it look a little better for us?" said Jack.

I kind of began to feel all scared up. "No, there's nothing I can do. What can I do? I don't even know what you've been doing."

I knew I could lighten the punishment of this pair by causing the documentary evidence to disappear, but the risk was too great; I should at least be reduced to the ranks and probably get court-martialed and sent to prison. Not worth it, said I to myself, oh no.

Arriving back at the docks, I reported myself and handed over the papers to the orderly sergeant. "Looks as if they've had a tough time, Corporal," remarked the sergeant to me. "Drunk I suppose as usual, better get them cleaned up a bit; the CO will be here in about half an hour. He'll dispense of this case as soon as he arrives."

The CO arrived, seating himself at a little table in one of the sheds. The adjutant was standing at his right and our company officer on his left. He was reading the evidence I'd brought from the detention barracks. Turning to the sergeant major, the CO said, "March the prisoners in." Peter and Jack were placed between an armed escort and marched to within a few feet in front of the table.

"Take their helmets off, Corporal," said the sergeant major, and I removed their headgear, taking up my position about two paces to the rear. Here Jack relaxed a little.

"Stand to attention!" roared the sergeant major. I could see that Peter was also shaking a bit in his pants but was trying to put on a brave front. The CO eyed them up and down for a second, then "Hmmm, two bright-looking specimens of humanity you look," he said. Then picking up the papers, he started to read very solemnly:

"N8334 J. Gibson and 8459 P. Harris, you are jointly charged with breaking out of the dockyard whilst on active service contrary to rules and regulations. Creating a disturbance in the city of Bombay. Using foul and abusive language to an NCO whilst in the execution of his duty. Being drunk.
Was apprehended by the military foot police about 12 midnight 5 November 1914."

The CO then read the evidence as follows:

To: The Officer Commanding 2nd Battalion Norfolk Regiment
*   Bombay Docks*
*   From: Sgt. O. Moore MFP Detention Barracks Bombay*

*   Sir:*
*   I was on duty in the vicinity of the Temple Bar, a saloon in Bombay, on the night of November 4 between 11 and 12 when I was requested by the proprietor of the saloon to try and stop a drunken disturbance in progress in his establishment between some soldiers and sailors, whom he had refused to serve. As I entered the door, I saw Private Harris with a chair uplifted in his*

hands, and he was about to swipe all the glasses from the counter. He was in a very excitable, drunken condition. Private Gibson, who appeared to be with him, was also very much the worse for liquor. I immediately arrested them and had them conveyed to the detention barracks. On the way, they used the most foul, abusive, and threatening language towards me and my escort. The saloon keeper estimated the damage done by the above men would cost between 200 and 300 rupees. This is my evidence; I swear it to be the truth, the whole truth, and nothing but the truth, so help me God.

I am, Sir,
Your Obedient Servant
O. Moore, Sgt.
Military Foot Police
5 November 1914

The CO glared up at them as if he was going to eat them up.

"This is a damn fine state of affairs, you pair of miserable jackasses, a disgrace to the regiment. What have you got to say to these most degrading charges? First of all, I want to know how, when, and what time did you get out of the dockyard?"

"Sir," began Peter. "We didn't get out at all, that's the truth. We got in, and the corporal here he come and let us out this morning early."

"What corporal?" roared the CO. "Where is he? Why isn't he here?"

"I think Harris has misunderstood you," said the sergeant major; then turning to Peter, the sergeant major said, "What the CO wants to know is *what time did you get out of the dockyard last night* and *how did you get out*? Now do you understand?"

"Yes, sir, I understand, but I don't seem to know much about it. I know we walked 'round the ships for a time; then we went on one of the ships and had a few drinks, me and Gibson here. Then we went 'round again 'til I thought we got back where we started from."

Then Peter started to scratch his head.

"Stand to attention," roared the sergeant major, "and speak up."

"Did you go out of one of the gates?" asked the CO.

"No, Sir."

"Did you climb over the wall?"

"No, Sir. I don't seem to remember much about it 'til we woke up in the cells this morning."

"Now Private Gibson, perhaps you can tell me how you came to get out of the dockyard last night?"

"Yes, Sir," began Jack. "It's like this, Sir, as Private Harris says, we had a few drinks with some friends; then we was coming back when we see a little boat tied upta one of the big ships and Private Harris here, he says how we had better go fer a little row around the docks and with that he slips over the side into the boat and cuts the rope. Then we both goes fer a little row and got out inter the sea, but somehow we can't get the boat ter go very good as we only had one oar. It was getting' dark, an' we couldn't find our way ter get back."

"Yes, what then?" asked the CO as Jack paused for a while.

"Then a motor boat came ter us and asked us if we wanted to go ashore, so they pulled us to the shore, and when we got up some steps, we was in the street."

"What did you do with the boat you had stolen?"

"Oh, we let that go, Sir."

"Is this the truth you're telling me, or is this some dream you're trying to make me believe?"

"No, Sir, it's the gospel truth so help me."

"Then what happened?" asked the CO.

"I don't remember quite all of it. You see, Sir, both of us was pretty well full up with whiskey, but I do know that we see some sailors, and they took us along with them to have a drink or two. Then we played cards for a few more drinks and so on, Sir, then Harris here like a bloody fool . . ."

"Stop that language," hissed the sergeant major.

"Beg pardon, Sir, beg pardon. Yes, Sir, as I was saying, Harris here gets to arguing with the sailors something about the superior branch of the service. The sailors sayed that they belong to the superior part of the service, but Harris said that sojers always come fust. That's how they kept on going until Harris gets a poke on the snitch; then somebody hit me on the back of the head, and then the hell started. We give 'em as much as we could, but there was about a dozen of them an' only two of us, so I think maybe we got the worst part of it."

"What then?" asked the CO.

"I dunno, Sir, but I think that is all there is. As far as I know. We was both locked up when we woke up this morning. But I'd thank you, Sir, not to be too hard on us 'cause I don't think it's all our fault."

"Do you plead guilty to being drunk?"

"No, Sir, I don't think I was drunk. Harris here, he might have been but not me."

"Do you admit that you had some whiskey and beer to drink?"

"Yes, Sir."

"How much did you drink?"

"Oh, maybe we had a bottle or two."

"Well, according to rules and regulations," went on the CO, "a man who admits only taking one glass of beer is drunk. Remember that in future. March them out for a few minutes, Sergeant Major."

"Prisoners and escort," roared the sergeant major, "about turn, right turn, quickly march, halt, stand easy."

The CO conferred with the adjutant and company officer for a while. Meanwhile, Peter and Jack were outside the shed all of a lather; the sweat was soaking through their khaki jackets."

"How about a drink now?" said Peter.

"Shut up," said the sergeant major.

After a little delay Peter and Jack were marched back in front of the CO.

"Will you take my punishment or be tried by court-martial?"

They both agreed to take the CO's punishment.

The CO said, "Privates Gibson and Harris. I have carefully considered your case and have come to the conclusion that you were both drunk and got mixed up in a drunken brawl with those sailors; apparently you were both drunk before leaving the dockyard as it has been proved, which is no excuse. Do you understand?"

"Yes, Sir," replied both Peter and Jack.

"These charges that have been brought against you are of a very serious nature according to King's rules and regulations."

"But Sir . . ." began Peter.

"Hold your tongue, Private Harris," shouted the sergeant major.

"But," continued the CO, "under the present conditions and taking into consideration your previous good character, I'm going to deal as leniently as I possibly can. You'll both forfeit 14 days' pay and pay the expenses, if any, which may arise from this case. March them out, Sergeant Major."

"Thank God that's over," said Jack, the sweat rolling down his face. "If that's Bombay, I don't want to set eyes on it again. Jesus, I thought I was going to get hung. Got any money, Peter? Come on. Let's hunt up a beer or I'll be dying very soon."

Mesopotamia

The bugle sounded the "fall in," the regiment formed up and filed up the gangways of the ship, the ropes were cast off, the ship was guided by a couple of powerful tugs, and the SS *Elephanta* was pulled out to sea with her nose pointed to the west. A native infantry band on the docks struck up "Soldiers of the Queen" and "Should Auld Acquaintance Be Forgot" as a parting shot to us. But our destination was still unknown to us; we appeared to be sailing under sealed orders. Besides our regiment, there was a few details from other British units and a few native troops on board. The tugs had let us go, and the pilot was leaving the ship, which was well underway, when a large tug was noticed coming full speed after us, tooting her whistle desperately, trying to draw our attention. She had on board about 100 ranks which had, in the hustle and bustle in getting away, been left behind. Ropes and ladders were thrown over the side, and those soldiers clambered aboard as best they could, being pulled over the side by willing hands. Bombay was gradually fading away as the ship gained speed and was soon lost to view.

"Thank holy Moses," said Peter. "I hope I've seen the last of that godforsaken country."

"Me, too," chirped in Jack. "Hellova country that is."

Night was just falling, and we prepared to spend our first night at sea in the Indian Ocean. That was the night of 6 November 1914.

Orders were issued that no lights or smoking was allowed after dark until further orders. It was whispered 'round that the German raider *Emden* commanded by Captain von Mueller was supposed to be in the vicinity. She had already shown up and had fired shells into Madras, set several oil tanks ablaze, captured several merchant ships, and sunk them after taking their coal and stores. She had been very successful as a raider, and we surely didn't feel any too comfortable with the thoughts of her lurking around. She was, however, finally trapped at Cocas Island by the Australian Navy warship *HMS Sidney*, and the captain and crew were taken prisoners of war (10 November 1914). But it surely didn't add to our comfort to know that she, at any moment, might pay us a surprise visit, and then down we'd go. After we'd been at sea three days, we heard of her capture with some relief.

Peter and Jack had been assigned to staff jobs. Jack was OC of the wash house; his duties were to have the wash house spic and span, ready for the captain's daily inspection of the ship. Jack could be heard every morning cussing somebody who wanted to use his wash house after he had got it all polished up.

"No, yer can't come in 'ere ter wash yer damn rotten sweaty socks nor anything else 'til after the inspection. What the hell do yer think I'm bin washing this 'ere damned place for? Now get going afore I jam this 'ere mop down yer throat. Don't forget I'm the OC here."

Peter was employed in the ship's bakery helping to make the daily bread. He could be seen stripped to the waist punching large pieces of dough, perspiring from head to toe. Jack happened to look in one morning.

"What are yer doing, Peter? Are yer trying to knock all the guts out of that bread?"

Peter straightened his back. "Now look, yer here, you thick-skinned son of a Norfolk farmer, an' listen to me. I'm going to tell yer that I did this 'ere kind of work afore your arse was as big as a shirt button and long afore I comed into the Army. Now goter hell; u'm getting extra pay fer doing this kinda work, an extra beer, too. Put that in yer pipe and smoke it."

For the first two or three days, we had lectures on what to do in case of alarm. Every man was supplied with a life belt and shown how to put it on in a hurry, what to do and how to act if we found ourselves in the water, etc. After we received the news of the *Emden*'s capture, we had lessons in the art of making knots and lashing rafts together, what to do in case of fire, and finally, learning how to assemble ourselves and prepare to abandon the ship.

The ship was very much overcrowded, and as there were no hammocks, we had to sleep in any old place on the docks. We never undressed, that is below the belt; the weather remained calm and very hot so we needed no covers. During the day, most of the men were grouped about playing cards. Very little exercise could be indulged in on account of the crowded nature of the ship. But under the conditions, the voyage was quite pleasant.

Two or three fellows were fooling around one day by the side of an open hatchway and one of them accidentally fell into the hatch and broke his neck. He was buried at sea the same day. His body was wrapped up in canvas and weighted with some iron. The parson (or "shy pilot" as he was generally known amongst the soldiers) read a burial service. The body was then discharged into the sea while a bugle sounded the last post. The ship had come to a standstill while the rituals were being performed. Peter, who had been watching the ceremony, said to me, "The war is over for that poor bugger; he's only the advance party gone to tell 'em the rest of us is on our way. Good luck ter him. I hope he pops in a good word for me."

We had been at sea about seven days when it was officially announced to us we were going to Mesopotamia to invade that country now occupied by the Turks and that we were now known as the 6th Poona Division Indian Expeditionary Force "D." Our present force consisted of the 2nd Norfolk and the 1st Dorsets (British units), two Indian native battalions, and a few mountain guns: a total strength of about 5,000. The Dorsets had already made a landing under the protection of the Navy guns which were to cooperate with us on the rivers. There was one small cruiser and two river sloops armed with small guns.

We were awakened one morning by the bugle sounding the reveille for the first time, and it made us feel as if we were back in barracks again. All was quiet, not even the familiar sound of the ship's engines, only just a slight rolling of the ship. On deck could be seen the reflection of the sun's rays just before it popped up on the horizon. Then we heard a band playing our regimental March Royal, "Rule Britannia," and away through the mist on our port side we could faintly distinguish the funnels and outline of a British cruiser. The boys clambered on deck and gave her a rousing cheer. Both ships were now moving slowly ahead; we were well up the Persian Gulf and about to enter the Shatt-al-Arab, a stretch of water which at that point separated the borders of Mesopotamia and Persia. The Shatt-al-Arab extended from the mouth of the Gulf to Kurna, a distance of about 50 miles, and was there joined by the rivers Euphrates and Tigris of Biblical fame.

We were delayed there for a few hours to wait for the tide to turn before we could cross the bar. In the meantime, small bags of sand were placed around the upper decks of the ship. Orders were then issued for all marksmen and first-class shots to lie behind those bags with rifles loaded. It was only a precautionary measure, as the 1st Dorset Regiment had already landed and was a few miles up the Shatt-al-Arab. Preceded by a sloop, we went on our way, leaving the cruiser to guard the entrance as she was too large to cross the bar. On the right bank, we passed the remains of a Turkish fort which the cruiser had destroyed, causing the small Turkish garrison to flee. Our process was very slow, owing to our having no pilot. Usually Arab pilots navigated ships on the Shatt-al-Arab, but the Arabs were under Turkish rule, so we had to feel our own way very slowly, which gave us a chance to study the nature of the country we were passing through. Both banks were lined with date palms, stretching back some 300 or 400 yards from the river.

Beyond those trees, there was nothing but the open desert. Large dikes and ditches could be seen that filled up with water on the rise of the tide. We passed several little groups of Arabs squatting amongst the

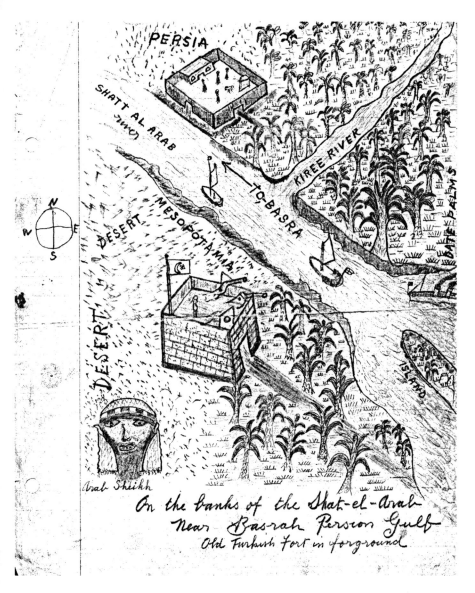

PERSIA

SHATT AL ARAB (river)

KIREE RIVER

TO BASRA

DESERT DESERT MESOPOTAMIA

DATE PALMS

ISLAND

Arab Sheikh

On the banks of the Shat-el-Arab
Near Basrah Persian Gulf
Old Turkish Fort in forground

trees. Some were armed with guns, but they made no signs; they just simply gazed at us as we passed on. There was no other life except for a few half-starved mongrel dogs which stared at us for a moment and then made off out of sight.

We anchored that night in the Shatt-al-Arab. A concert was organized; the best singers were rounded up. A free issue of beer was served out. Tobacco and cigarettes were freely distributed amongst the men, and everybody appeared to be having a good time. Peter sang about the only song he knew:

Poor old Patrick Finnegan
He grew whiskers on his chin again
The wind came up and blew them in again
Poor old Patrick Finnegan.

Then Jack, who was by this time slightly illuminated, presented himself at the piano with his version of boozing songs:

Goodbye booze fer evermore
My boozing days are almost o'
I've had a good time you will agree
But look what booze 'as done fer me.
        [Chorus]
An' when I dies don't bury me atall
Just pickle me bones in alcohol
Put a bottle of booze at me head an' feet
An' then I know I'm sure to keep."

That was the last time poor old Jack sang that song. Before many more hours had passed, he was dead. Shot through the head in our first engagement with the Turks. What a good thing it was we couldn't see what was ahead of us. After all, what was a soldier but common fodder?

By sunrise the next morning we were on the move, and after two hours steaming, I saw a flag signaler calling up and reading his message as he flagged it through in Morse code. He said, "GOC advance no further; land here. OC Dorsets," which meant that we were at the end of our voyage. We had been ten days at sea.

No time was lost to preparing to get ashore. With the help of the Navy's boats and our own, we were all ashore in a few hours. We had some difficulty on account of the steep banks and had to be hauled up with the help of ropes and ladders, which caused us lots of fun, many of us getting a dunking in the water.

The Capture of Basra

We were greeted by the boys of the Dorset Regiment. They had been doing outpost work, waiting two days for us. They told us all they knew: that they had landed at Fao just after the sailors had silenced the Turkish fort but hadn't yet come in contact with the enemy and that there was a hostile force entrenched a few miles away. We were at once ordered to dig trenches sufficiently deep enough to give us some head cover in case of possible attack. The ground was soft and sandy which made the work easy. After sentries had been posted and other necessary duties attended to, we were permitted to light fires and make some tea. We had nothing to cook as our rations consisted of bully beef and biscuits.

Towards the evening we had a lecture from our company officer who told us something about the nature of the country. It was inhabited chiefly by wild Arab tribes, and their only occupation was to rob and plunder each other. He said that we were going to move off just before daybreak the following morning and that we should probably be engaged by the enemy. They were rotten shots and weren't used to the tactics of modern warfare as we knew it; from information we'd received, their arms and ammunition were obsolete, and they were an irregular force composed of a mixture of Arab and a few Turkish regulars. It was also known that they had a few small guns and were entrenched a few hours' march from our position on the right bank of the river. The orders were that if "any of you fellows get wounded, one man is to stay with him until picked up by the stretcher bearers who will follow in the rear." Our main object was to capture the city of Basra about 20 miles by the river.

After the lecture, our platoon sergeant gave us a little advice. He was an old soldier, having been through the Boer War:

"I want to tell some of you youngsters that I happen to know something about these dark-skinned blaggards they call Arabs. They are the most ferocious barbarous villains under God's sun. They always have a notion that they're fighting a holy war, that murder, thieving, and plunder is all part of their religion, and that to die on the battlefield means going to heaven for them. In large numbers they'll fight fanatically and put up a brave front, but individually they haven't the guts of a louse. My advice to you youngsters is this: If by any chance you get into a tight corner where they're concerned, use your ammunition sparingly and make every shot tell. If you find you're losing out, don't forget to save a round of ammunition for yourself; for God's sake don't fall into their hands alive. No, I'm not kidding. Don't think I am. A joke's all right in its place, but we happen to be past the joking stage right now. You can believe me. They give no quarter nor respect."

I could see Peter sitting there with his topi balanced on the back of his head, his mouth wide open, and his eyes nearly sticking out of his head.

"Blimey," said Jack to me. "He's a cheerful sort of bugger. Sounds as if we was going ter have a real day tomorrow here. Corporal, do yer believe all what that cockeyed sergeant said?"

"I don't know, Jack. You know just about as much as I do. Maybe we'll soon find out for ourselves." I picked up my helmet which I'd placed on top of the trench and was about to place it on my head when I noticed two funny-looking creatures about two inches long.

"What do you call these?" I asked the sergeant who was standing by.

"Don't touch them for chrissake. They're a couple of black scorpions; their sting is nearly as deadly as a cobra bite. Give your helmet to me."

He shot them on the ground and stamped them out.

"Good thing you didn't put it on your head," he said. "There may be lots of them in this country. We had plenty of them in South Africa. Damn nasty things."

"Hello, Jack, what's the matter? You look as if you'd lost something. Anything wrong?"

"No, Corporal. I was just thinking an' thinking an' thinking."

"What are you thinking about? Surely you're not worried about getting your first taste of fire tomorrow?"

"Yes, Corporal. That's jes what I'm thinking about. Come over here and sit down. I've got something ter tell yer."

I followed Jack into a trench, wondering what was on his mind.

"I want to ask yer, Corporal, ter do me a favour."

"Why, of course, Jack," I replied; "If it's in my power, depend on me."

"Well, listen ter me, Corporal. I've been sort of kind o' worried since we started from India. First of all, Corporal, do you believe in fortune tellers? You know what I mean, them old Indian fakirs who can do all kinds of mysterious tricks way back in India."

"I know what you mean, Jack, I've seen them many times, and they certainly seem to be very clever."

"Well now, listen ter what I'm going to tell yer. About two weeks before we left India, me and Peter went to the bull ring to see our gal. She was 'bout the nicest gal in the bull ring. Her name is Nel-a. Maybe you know her. Me and Peter used to go and see her every pay day. Well, the last time we see her, we told her how we was going to the war. She seemed ter be all cut up about it and started ter cry like some little kid. We sort o' kidded her up a bit. She gits up, tells us to 'bitha attora,' slips out the door, comes back with a bottle of whiskey an' a few bottles of beer, and tells us to help ourselves. Of course, we was tickled to death. We both enjoyed ourselves with her, and she wouldn't take a penny. Then she asked us if we would like to have our fortune told before we went to war. 'That's jus' what I want,' says Peter, 'and me, too' says I although I never believe much in this fortune-telling stuff. It seems kinda all nonsense to me. But just to oblige, we told her to go ahead. 'No, sahib,' she says. 'You must go to the old temple which stands back on the Ramghat Road.' You know that old temple, Corporal, where we used ter go sometimes on baksheesh days? It's near Tiger Hill."

"Yes, I know, Jack. Go on."

"Well, she says fer us to be there the next day about an hour afore the sun go down. 'All right, Nel-a,' we ses. 'We'll be there.' Then she seemed pleased with herself and takes all her clothes off and does a kind o' cancan dance. She sure was a great kid, the best-hearted native I ever did come across, an' as clean as a new pin. She then takes off two little bells from the ring that was 'round her ankle, gives one ter me and t'other to Peter, and told us ter keep that bell fer luck 'til we come back from the war."

"Next day we goes ter the temple as she said, and after a while we sees a tonga coming up the road. Nel-a got out with one of them funny little old native men. He was all skin an' bone; his legs was not much fatter than a blooming match, an' he kinda hobbled along. He went inter the temple and beckoned us to follow him. He said, 'Salaam, sahib, you know Nel-a, sahib. I know all.' He could speak our lingo better than us. 'Nel-a tells me you're going away to the war and would like to have your fortune told. I possess that power, sahib, but I only tell the truth, sahib. I cannot lie; it is beyond my power to lie, sahib. I tell only what you can see for yourself, so you see that I cannot lie some. You may see something, sahib, that is not favourable to you, sahib; then you may become angry with me, sahib, but I cannot help it, sahib, for it is the truth. I am very old man. I was very old man before your father was born and his father before him. I shall be very old man, sahib, after you are gone.'

'For chrissake,' said Peter, 'yer must be older than Noah. Where the hell did yer come? Yer look like as if yer come out of the blooming ark, for chrissake. Get on with the job.'

'You must have patience, sahib, and it is bad to curse, sahib. I can only tell your future if you will not be angry with me at what you see, sahib. You must promise because my great observation powers never fail. People come to me, sahib, because I never lie. Let me show you something, sahib. Please close the temple door.'

Peter closed the heavy door and left us in darkness.

'Now watch, sahib.'

Very slowly the door began to open but not from where the latch was. Instead, the door opened from the side where the hinges were.

'You see, sahib, some of the power I possess. Keep still, sahib; the door will close again.' The door returned to its place.

'Now please open the door,' said the old fakir.

Peter pushed the door open and examined it but could see nothing unusual.

'I dunno, but you must be Jesus Christ himself,' says Peter.

'No, sahib, I show you this as an example of my unusual power.'

'Now, sahib, I will proceed to tell you your future.' From a little box he takes two pair of coloured glasses and a little glass bottle half full of some kind of water. He then drops something into the bottle and stirs it up with a stick, and the water gives off a kind of a blue smoke. This he places between me and hisself. I kinda gets winded up and was going ter get up, but he says, 'Keep quite still, sahib.' Then he gives me a pair of glasses and tells me ter put them on. He puts the other pair on. Then he gits hold of my left hand with his right.

'Now, sahib,' he says, 'look straight into my eyes and tell me what you see. Do you see that black line moving, sahib? Yes, that is a train, sahib; you are in that train. The scene changes; do you see a large city, sahib?'

'Yes,' says Jack.

'There is now water and large clouds above the water. Do you see it, sahib?'

'Yes, yes.'

'There is a big ship; do you see the ship, sahib?'

'Yes, I can see it quite good.'

'You are in that ship, sahib,' says the old man.

I then saw a man running and then fall down. I saw a flash, and the glasses got darker.

'Did you see the fire, sahib? That is the fire that accompanies the rain that God sends.'

Then I saw a man running again and then appears to fall down again. He gets up again but falls almost immediately. Then the glasses grew dark. I could see no more.

'Did you see that man, sahib? That man is you, sahib. There is nothing more coming, sahib. That is all. The glasses told you the truth be prepared.'

The old man then wanted to tell Peter his fortune, but he got sorta scared and said he had heard enough."

"Now tell me, Corporal, what do yer think about that? It's kinda got hold of me. You see, Corporal, everything the old man said seems to be true except the last part which is ter come. Seems sorta funny, don't it?"

"I wouldn't let that bother you, Jack. The old man knew you was going to the war. He knew you would have to go by train and ship. I don't believe in those old fakirs. Forget all about it."

"Well, Corporal," says Jack, "I want yer to do the favour I spoke about. If anything happens to me tomorrow, you know what I mean, I want yer to write a letter to my mother and tell her all about it. If yer will do this, that's all I want, and good luck to yer, Corporal."

The nights in Mesopotamia were very cold at that time of year. Each man carried one blanket and one waterproof sheet. We made ourselves as comfortable as possible: Some coiled up in their own blankets; others shared their blankets and made one big bed. But there was very little sleep for any of us. We heard what appeared to be a few rifle shots away in the distance; otherwise, all was perfectly quiet, the calm before the storm.

We were aroused long before daybreak. Hot tea was already made for us, and we made a hasty meal of biscuits and tea. We formed up by companies in columns of fours, myself, Jack, and Peter being in one column, slowly marched out to the open desert, and formed up again in column of double companies. In this formation, the advance began. The sun came up in all its glory and soon warmed us up. After an hour's march, a ten-minute halt was called, enabling us to look around a bit although there was nothing particular to see. Away to the west was nothing but miles of open desert, not a sign of life to be seen; to the west could be seen the date palms that lined the river banks. We then formed up in echelon formation and started to advance again. The going was slow and hard on account of the sand. It was no joke marching through sand up to the tops of our boots. On our right and near the date trees was the Dorsets and on our left a native regiment. In the rear was a few details, another native regiment, and a battery of small guns. That comprised our little army. The Navy sloops were advancing on the river; in advance of us some 600 yards was a screen of scouts. We had been marching about five hours when we heard the well-known whistle of a shell traveling through the air and then a loud explosion.

"What the hell was that?" cried Peter. *Bang, bang, bang.* They began to come over pretty fast. "Deploy outwards from the centre," came the order.

Every man moved into position like clockwork, and before many seconds, our army was one long, single line. Most of the shells were bursting to the rear of us, doing little damage. We advanced until we came up in line with the scouts who were under rifle fire. We could now see the enemy trenches some 800 yards ahead. We then started to advance by sections of about 12 men by short rushes. Our gunners had now got the range and were pouring shells over our heads as fast as they could. We could also hear the Navy blasting away at the enemy. We had now come within rifle range of the enemy. I could hear the whistle of the bullets passing through the air. The battle was now in full blast. Rapid fire came from one platoon sergeant; 12 paces rush came from another. Then again my section, 12 paces rush, rapid fire.

"Go boys, let them have it."

The enemy bullets were kicking up the sand everywhere. Just at that time the clouds burst, and a storm the likes of which I've never experienced before broke over us as if a part of a great drama. In a few seconds, we were wet to the skin, but advance we must. Orders were heard with difficulty. We could rush only two or three paces before sinking exhausted to the ground. The lightning flashed overhead, and the thunder roared worse than a million guns. The sand had become a clammy substance and clung to our shoes in heavy clods. Men were cussing from being blinded. I could see the wounded and dead lying around behind us. By now we were all mixed up in other sections. I could see Jack just ahead of me, and I made an effort to catch up with him. I saw him get up, about to make another short rush, when I saw his rifle leave his hands and saw him fall back on his haunches. I knew he'd been hit. I crawled up to where he was, pulled his legs out, and got him on his back. The blood was coming from his head near his left temple. I took an old rag from my haversack to stop the flow.

"No good, Corporal; I've got it. Give me a drink of water."

I held my water bottle to his lips.

"Don't forget, Corporal; you know that favour."

He then coughed up a lot of blood and then rolled over. Poor old Jack had gone. At that moment, the colonel and adjutant came up. The colonel, I noticed, had two bullet holes in the top of his helmet.

"Is he wounded?" he asked me.

"I believe he has just passed away, Sir," I replied.

"Get on, get on," he said. "It's too warm. We're right in the range here. Try and catch up with the line."

The storm had ceased as suddenly as it had begun. Most of our rifles had now become jammed, owing to the sand clogging up the bolts.

We were about 200 yards from the trenches when the bugle sounded the charge. The boys were up and with a roar we went like hell for those trenches. Most of the enemy were now flying for their lives as fast as their legs could go, leaving everything behind them. Thank God the battle was over; never shall I forget it. We were all in. The artillery were still sending shells after the fleeing enemy; most of them returned carrying white flags. As for us, we were too exhausted to take much notice of anything: miserably wet through and covered with dirt. Although we appeared to be fairly happy, nobody was singing. The enemy didn't seem to have a very formidable force, good for us. Although we didn't know their actual strength, they had the advantage over us. We were advancing over a surface as flat as a billiard table, not so much as a blade of grass to take cover behind, handicapped by the mud and sand which clung to our shoes like large clods of dough and eventually clogging the mechanism of our rifles. Lucky for us the end came when it did. Lucky, too, for us the enemy had no machine guns because I could plainly see it would have been goodbye to our expeditionary force. Scattered over the battlefield could be seen the dead and wounded.

After a brief rest, the prisoners which numbered about 500 were marched away to our rear. Shovels were given them to go out and bury their dead where they lay. Our stretcher bearers were busy collecting our wounded and carrying them to the river where they were placed aboard the ship which had followed up the river. Volunteers were called for to go out and bury our dead. Our casualties were roughly between 300 and 500. We formed up and retired about a mile to the edge of the palm trees. On the way we passed the general, who was on horseback standing by a flagpole flying the Union Jack. He had his hand up at the salute. Here we all buckled to. Some went to the ship to get meat, potatoes, and bread; others made fires for cooking; and after a good meal we felt little the worse for our experience. After a while, Peter turned up. He had been to the dressing station to have a slight flesh wound attended to. Somehow he had managed to stop one in the fleshy part of his hindquarters.

"How come you got it there? Was you trying to run away?" I asked him.

"You blimey! I don't know, Corporal. The doctor said it looked like one of our own bullets; maybe someone behind me took me for a blooming Arab. What about Jack? Where is he?" asked Peter. "Did he get one, too?"

When I told him, he cried like a kid. "Poor old Jack! Me and him come from the same town. We knowed each other since we was kids together, we enlisted together, and figured on going home together. To hell with this war. I wonder what his poor old mother will do. He used to send her nearly all his pay. Funny thing, Corporal, some old fakir in India told him he'd get killed in the war. Seems very strange to me, Corporal, but it might have been me or you. Wonder any of us is alive in all that hell. What you think, Corporal?"

"It surely was going tough for us for a little while, but thank God it's all over."

"Wonder what we do next?" said Peter.

That night the wind blew up a bitter cold hurricane. Our blankets hadn't arrived, so we dug up heaps of sand to ward off the wind and cuddled up to each other to try and keep warm. We didn't need any rocking; sleep just came to us. I awoke once or twice, feeling cold, and heard a shot or two and the whistle of a bullet as it flew overhead. Evidently, there was a few snipers about.

Next morning we were all pleased to see the sun come up. It was never more appreciated as we were stiff with cold, but about midday the sun got unbearable, the temperature often being 100° to 140° in the shade. That day we were permitted to rest with the exception of a few special duties that had to be attended to. Food was taken to men on outpost duty. Some of the dead bodies had been unearthed by Arab prowlers and dogs. The bodies were buried again, but on account of the watery nature of the ground, it was impossible to dig deeper than about three feet down.

Me and a party of about 50 men were sent out to see if we could round up some of the snipers which continued to worry us. Apparently they were in hiding amongst the date palms. After proceeding about two miles we came upon a tent.

"Be careful how you approach that tent," said our officer.

Inside we found three wounded Turkish officers. We took their revolvers and swords. That tent was full of rifle ammunition which we dumped into the creeks. The officers seemed pleased to see us although we couldn't converse with them. We could see they were in a bad way. They made motions pointing to their wounds bandaged up with some old rags. Close by we found their horses: two small ponies already saddled as these fellows were too bad to walk. We got two of them in one saddle and sent them back to our camp; the other fellow rode his own horse. We continued our search but couldn't locate any snipers although every now and then we could hear shots. A little farther ahead we came upon some Arab shacks surrounded by a mud wall about ten feet high. Each hut had one small opening for a doorway. We cautiously entered only to find a few old Arab men and women who glared at us in a strange way but didn't speak or molest us in any way.

We searched the place but found no arms of any kind. There were some tons of dates all stored in large, covered shacks, as well as chickens, young calves, and cows. We took some chickens and eggs; some of the boys collared a young calf. We filled our pockets full of dates and returned to camp well pleased with the day's work. That night we were busy stewing chickens, a change from the ordinary Army rations. Our transport had arrived with our blankets, etc. We then heard that the general had sent orders to the Turkish commander in Basra that if he

Arab Chiefs

didn't surrender the city within 24 hours, we were going to bombard the city and set it on fire.

Next day a party of horsemen arrived under a white flag. The outpost party brought them in. Soon we heard the news: The Turks had evacuated, taking all their equipment with them, and the people of Basra were sending river steamers to convey us to the city.

The Port of Basra

The next morning, we boarded river steamers used for trade purposes between Basra and Baghdad, some 500 miles apart as the River Tigris flows. The steamers had two decks and could accommodate about 500 troops in a standing position; they were of the paddle-wheel and stern-wheel type, built for shallow draft, and could be handled by a crew of four men. On the Tigris proper and on account of the swift-flowing and treacherous nature of the river, ships proceeding upstream had to give way to ships coming down in order to avoid collisions.

We passed the Hamerdan and the Anglo-Persian Oil Company's works on the left bank. A little farther ahead we passed a large steamer called the *Akbar* which was partly submerged by the Turks to bar our way. On the Persian side, we passed a smart-looking building which had a couple of small guns mounted in the garden; we were told that was a palace belonging to the sheikh of Muhommerah, whoever he was. There was nothing very attractive except for a few Arab huts situated in the midst of the everlasting date trees. Arriving at Basra, the ship made fast to an old wooden jetty which looked as if it was about to collapse. The banks were lined with big, ugly-looking Arab junks. All was very quiet on shore; we saw only a few men dressed in European clothes, wearing Turkish hats, who we learned were English and American merchants representing their firms in this out-of-the-way city of Sinbad the sailor. We clambered ashore and were housed in the warehouses along the river front. The officers were greeted by Sir Percy Cox, the British commissioner in Basra, and his wife. It was due to his diplomacy that the city had been saved from a bombardment. That night we were strictly confined to our quarters, which were overrun with rats and full of flies, mosquitoes, and numerous other crawling insects.

The following day buildings were taken over for military purposes; guards and sentries were posted at important points in the city placed under martial law. My regiment took over the old Turkish barracks, a large building about 300 yards square, and prepared to settle down to ordinary military life. For a few days, we weren't permitted to go out in the city except on duty. There was no way of getting out of those barracks, only through the one gate where the guard room was bolted. All the windows of the soldiers' quarters were heavily barred; the doors opened only onto the parade ground. Our quarters looked more like a prison. The Turks had left nothing of importance but a lot of filth.

After a day or two, the inhabitants began to come out. Shops and stores opened up and were doing good business especially among the troops. The city was flooded with beer, wines, and spirits. Beer from Germany, wines from France, and whiskeys from Scotland and all of the genuine article. Such abundance of alcohol may seem strange because the religious nature of the population prohibited use of that product.

Basra was composed of two parts separated by a creek: One part was called Ashar, the other Old Basra. The creek was also known as Ashar Creek. That creek was the outlet for all the filth and slime of the city and was carried away to the Shatt-al-Arab. By the rise and fall of the tides, the creek was altogether an unsanitary, unhealthy, stinking hole, and yet that creek was the city's main water supply. The water was carried away in small earthenware vessels on the heads of women, a practice so common in the East. The population which might be anything from 50,000 to 100,000 people were composed of a mixed crowd. There was to be found in that city dark-skinned Nubians, Egyptians, Arabs, Persians, Armenians, Greeks, and Turks. It was truly interesting to any newcomer to watch that mixed crowd of humanity in their native costumes of various colours. The general language spoken was Arabic. Little children were running around stark naked, their dirty little faces a playground for multitudes of flies. The streets were full of half-starved beggars scantily clothed, asking for baksheesh. The houses were flat roofed and built of clay brick. Most of the traffic was done in bellams and small boats on the numerous creeks which abounded the city. Arab boatmen plying for hire and fighting to get a fare, people coming and going. But nobody seemed to be doing anything in particular. Could all these people make a living from the date harvest? There was nothing modern. The place was as ancient as it was when Moses ruled.

It was soon discovered that Basra was rife with disease and full of syphilis; about every other door was a brothel. The women plied their trade openly even to the extent of riding around the creeks in bellams. Before long, some of the soldiers were affected by that terrible disease and immediately shipped back to India. We were lectured by the medical officers about venereal disease. It was painted in all its colours and various stages and warned for the benefit of ourselves to keep away from the women. It was estimated that 50 percent of the men and women were suffering from the disease in some form or other. The authorities did all they possibly could to clamp the lid down: The city was flooded with military police who had orders to arrest any soldier seen leaving a private residence, merchants were forbidden under pain of severe penalty to serve any soldier with intoxicants with the exception of a few special well-conducted stores owned by Europeans, but their supplies were soon exhausted by the thirsty Tommies. Soon Basra was as dry as a bone.

To the north of the city was an Arab cemetery which couldn't be approached to within about 500 yards on account of the stench. The Arabs never dug a grave as we do, but lay their dead on the ground and build a canopy over the body with a mixture of clay and sand baked hard by the heat of the sun, so that the body reposed in a kind of small cave. A small opening big enough to put a hand in was made at the head, and to this opening was brought food and placed inside for the dead person to eat. Strange as it might seem, that practice was perfectly true. Such was the condition of that deplorable city as we found it at the later end of 1914 under Turkish administration.

The climate at that time of the year (November) was about at its best. It was extremely hot from about midday until after sundown, the nights turning very cool. Our greatest pests were the millions of flies which continually tormented us. At night we couldn't sleep for mosquitoes and sand flies, besides all the other crawling, creeping, and jumping creatures which the country was infested with. Sleep came only through sheer exhaustion, and on awakening, we looked more like spotted leopards from the bites of those miserable creatures. We soon found out that we weren't fighting only a war but were also fighting all kinds of diseases. Several of the soldiers became stricken with the disease diagnosed as beriberi, which showed itself by swelling of the feet and legs. Other were attacked with dysentery without warning and died within a few hours. At that time, hospital facilities and doctors were very inadequate. We were in a strange country never before entered by British soldiers. All drinking water was boiled and then filtered through large earthenware chathes and chlorinated before it was fit to drink.

The Battle for Kurna

We were nicely settled down and began to think that the war was over as far as we were concerned but no such luck. Orders were issued one night that we were to parade at daybreak and move up the Shatt-al-Arab to attack and drive out a Turkish force strongly entrenched about one mile south of Kurna, a village situated on the banks of the two rivers Euphrates and Tigris which met at that point and flowed as one into the Shatt-al-Arab. Kurna, often spoken of as the site of the original Garden of Eden of Biblical fame, was about 20 miles from Basra and 50 miles from the mouth of the Persian Gulf. Well, thinking that Basra was no place for respectable soldiers, our little force boarded the river steamers and other floating craft and were towed to as near as we dare go to the enemy's positions on the left bank of the Tigris opposite Kurna. We felt a little more secure because we had been reinforced with a battery of artillery with 18-pounders which had recently arrived from India. Basra had been left in the care of a few native soldiers until such time as reinforcements might arrive.

Under cover of darkness, our little force made a safe landing, having a little trouble getting the guns ashore. We were in the best of spirits and fairly fresh, having had no hard sands to march over. We crept up within about 600 yards of the enemy before they were aware of our existence. I don't think they were really expecting us, and we caught them "with their hair down," as the soldier says. We lay down in the sand in extended formation, scarcely daring to breathe, waiting for the dawn to break. How some of us would just have loved to have a smoke during that interval; the suspense of waiting was terrible. Gradually, the dawn was breaking in the east. It wouldn't be long now. All at once, without any warning, the enemy opened up with a rain of rapid fire, but they didn't have the range; their bullets were going high, well over our heads. Now was our chance. We had their range fairly accurate. Our whole front line returned their fire with a continuous hail of rapid fire. Our machine gunners were just sweeping them out of their trenches. Our advance had commenced. By continuous short rushes we were gradually nearing their positions, and before very long we could see them on the run towards the river. We were so excited that we didn't wait for any more orders; we fixed our bayonets and went after those Turks like greased lightning. Lots of them surrendered, and some got away in boats to the other side of the river where it was impossible for us to follow.

It was a decisive victory for us. The battle was over in about a couple of hours. Our casualties were practically nil, and the enemy had left two big guns behind with lots of rifles and ammunition. Their trenches were full of dead and wounded. Their condition was terrible to look at. There was great big Arabs and Turks literally torn to pieces, arms and legs badly damaged, some with their whole intestines hanging out. The sight made me feel sick. What kind of ammunition could have done all that dreadful work? I knew our gunners were practically firing point blank into them. Their groans and cries were pitiful to hear. Never before had I witnessed such a sight. If that was war, I was sick of it; I hoped it wouldn't fall to my lot to see it again. Yet there were others glorified at the sight, and right there and then I swore that I'd never fire another round with the purpose of hitting anyone. I heard afterwards that artillery had used an explosive called TNT; whatever that might be, I had no idea.

Later in the day we had the job of burying the dead in the trenches where they were killed. We just covered them up with the loose sand forming the parapet which was all we could do as they weren't in a condition to be handled. What an end to come to. I was by no means a saint, but that sort of thing got me thinking. Why had those poor devils suffered and what for? What was their reward? I had no business to complain because I was a professional soldier and that was what I enlisted for, but I supposed there were limits even in wars. While I was thus meditating, Peter came along.

"Hello, Corporal. I see you're all here. How goes it?"

After telling Peter my views, he said, "What in the name of Jesus is gone wrong with you? Why, you must be nutty or something. Don't you know that these sons of bitches would do the same to you and a damn sight more? Why, these beggars would cut your balls out if you ever give 'em the chance. Come on, let's try and get something to eat. You must be suffering from an empty stomach; you'll feel better after. Think of poor old Jack. He got no mercy. You must be getting homesick. We'll have to send you home to your mammy."

We collected all the rifles and ammunition which were afterwards dumped into the river. Most of those rifles were of a modern pattern and bore the name of a well-known German firm. The enemy had evidently been prepared for a long stand because provisions such as the Arabs eat were plentiful; they had enough dates packed in large wooden boxes to keep them for a year. After we had cleaned up the battlefield, we were permitted to rest. All the time small groups of the enemy were surrendering themselves. Our object hadn't yet been reached. Kurna lay on the other side of the Tigris where the enemy had now established themselves, and before we could take that place, other plans would have to be made. All that night the enemy harassed us with shellfire, doing no damage other than keeping us awake. The following morning all was quiet. The shelling had ceased. We waited for orders, wondering what the next move was going to be like.

Later in the morning, a party was seen approaching our camps, bearing a large white flag. That group turned out to be the sheikh of Kurna who had his little son with him, a boy about 12 years old. I don't think I'd ever seen such a beautiful picture of boyhood before in all my life. He was dressed in a spotlessly white costume, trimmed at the edges in a wonderfully worked gold lace. His headdress was of the ordinary Arab pattern but everywhere trimmed with gold. Under his outer garment he wore a gold decorated belt. Attached to it was one of the most beautiful little swords I'd ever seen: It had a jeweled handle and a case of solid silver, and the blade was inscribed with the most beautiful designs. On the other side of his belt he wore a funny ancient-looking dagger in a jeweled case. Shining in the sunlight, his face was a nut brown colour with large black eyes and eyelashes over a half-inch long. All the boys admired the little fellow.

The sheikh had brought us news that the Turks had fled up the Tigris and that he was prepared to surrender Kurna and afford us the use of all the river craft available to transport our troops across. His offer was gratefully accepted, and before very long the Union Jack was flying over the Garden of Eden. We had now penetrated some 120 miles into Mesopotamia.

We lost no time in crossing the Tigris and established ourselves about 1,000 yards above Kurna. It was there that we began to settle down. Rumours were going around that we'd reached the extent of our advance, and it certainly looked like it. We were set to work building up strong fortifications. Gun emplacements were made to accommodate our guns, earthworks were thrown up all around the encampment, and around outside a large creek was built which soon filled with water.

At that point, the cultivation of the date trees ceased. The river was no longer tidal beyond that point, making it difficult to irrigate the land. From our position there was nothing to be seen but the great open space of the Arabian desert. We couldn't expect any further assistance from the Navy; their ships drew too much water for them to proceed any farther, so they just threw out their anchors and stood by. We were allowed to visit the village only in groups, armed with rifles and ammunition with an NCO in charge. Plundering was forbidden and would be severely punished; every purchase was to be paid for in cash. The Arabs were never allowed near our camp. Kurna was only a small village of about 2,000 or 3,000 inhabitants.

Peter had been to the village and bought some chicken and eggs.

"Hi, Corporal," he hollered at me. "If that's the Garden of Eden, I wonder what the Garden of Hell is looking like. That's some damn garden if yer like. I wouldn't be seen dead in it. No wonder Adam and Eve pinched the fruit. They musta wanted to get out of it."

The old sheikh and his son would visit us almost daily, but they never came into the camp. For a few nights we were troubled by bands of hostile Arabs who would advance to within about 200 yards of our defenses, open a rapid fire for a few minutes, and then disappear as quickly as they came. Although we returned their fire, nothing was ever seen of them the following morning, neither dead nor wounded, although several of our boys received wounds from their fire. To stop the nuisance, an outpost was put out on a small sand hill about 500 yards from our defenses and was in telephone communication with the camp. The outpost was relieved every 24 hours and became known as Norfolk Hill. Two or three attacks were made on this outpost, but several of the enemy got entangled in the barb wire and were shot which put an end to their little tricks, and they bothered no more. In the daytime we could see large gatherings of them waving all kinds of coloured banners, but they always kept well out of the range of our guns.

Christmas Day found us in our encampment. Parcels had arrived from the ladies of India containing Xmas puddings, cake, candy; cheese, coffee, and tea; a supply of cigarettes and tobacco; and to cap it all, a free issue of rum. The boys got together in little groups. Songs were sung, mingled with Xmas carols. We were really better off than if we had been back in India. We were getting all the luxuries free of charge. What more did we desire?

Reinforcements began to arrive. The Oxford and Bucks light infantry took up a position on the opposite bank of the Tigris. Two powerful searchlights were set up in the emplacements. A native field bakery had arrived and was turning out nice new loaves of bread, something which we had almost forgotten about, and believe me, it was appreciated by all of us. Some six-inch guns replaced our 18-pounders, and we began to make ourselves very much at home. Peter didn't feel quite satisfied; he said that they ought to send the bull ring out, and then it would be a pretty good Garden of Eden.

We were now continually strengthening our position against any possible attack and were one day doing some repair work to one of the searchlight emplacements. We chanced to be looking in at the little

engine room which had been fitted up when a tall, smart-looking officer appeared in the doorway, wearing the badge of the Royal Engineers.
I thought he was going to ask me what my business was, but instead he
wished me good morning. I saluted him and said, "Good morning, Sir."

He then asked me how I was, how did I like the climate, how long
had I been out there, and what did I think of the game, etc. I knew it
was rather unusual for an officer to approach one of the rank and file in
such a familiar manner. We chatted on for a while; then he told me he
was the OC of the searchlight section and asked me if I knew anything
about searchlights. I told him that I had no particular knowledge about
searchlights but had a little experience with dynamos, generators, and
internal combustion engines. He questioned me to some extent on the
subject and seemed entirely satisfied with my answers. He then asked
me how I'd like to become attached to his section with additional pay.
Well, I just jumped at the opportunity. I was getting tired of digging. It
would be kind of a change anyway. So I told him that if he thought my
services were any good, I'd be very glad to serve him. He took my name
and number and said that I should probably hear from him sometime
tomorrow. He then wished me good morning and departed in the direction of our orderly room tent.

The next morning, sure enough I was ordered to appear before my
company officer. He just told me to pack my kit and report myself to the
OC searchlight section for duty, telling me to see my colour sergeant if I
needed any pay. I packed up, received my pay, said goodbye to the boys,
and was very soon with my new pals.

Those I found to be a jolly crowd, about a dozen all told. A mixture
of English, Irish, and Scotch, they were all volunteers and mechanics
from the large cities of India. Captain Stace, the OC, also a volunteer,
was an official employed in the mint at Bombay. None of them were very
much acquainted with military discipline; on the contrary, they seemed
to treat the whole matter as a huge joke. Like ours, their first experience
of actual service. They had, they told me, offered their services for various reasons: Some of them had been involved in scandals, a couple of
them had gotten mixed up with Eurasian families and had been forced
to marry and were glad of the means of getting separated from their
matrimonial ties, others had become so involved in debt that enlisting
was their only chance of ever getting away from India ("just one step
better than committing suicide" as they put it). All those young fellows
had left the old country to take positions in India some years before.

For the first few days I was trained in the way to handle the lights,
which was a very simple matter. All I had to know was how to elevate,

depress, and transverse the beam so as to pick up objects and hold them in the beam as a target. Every night after dark and throughout the night at about half-hour intervals, those lights were switched on and concentrated over the desert. Wild dogs and jackals would stare into the beam, their eyes shining like balls of fire. Sometimes in the distance we would pick up a line of camels on the march. Those lights no doubt proved effective in keeping away the raiding parties of Arabs. It relieved the outposts, who were called in. The troops would gather round and want to know what time the "picture show" opened.

By that time, we were on friendly terms with the inhabitants of Kurna, and I think they were quite pleased to have us there. They supplied us with all kinds of fresh vegetables, besides chickens, ducks, and eggs. They had never done such good business since the days of Solomon. The womenfolk, their faces always concealed so we couldn't say whether they were pretty or otherwise, would come to the river to get water and do their washing. The men would spend most of the day sitting outside tea shops under an old patched-up canopy, sipping tea out of very small glasses.

A company of sappers and miners had arrived and built a pontoon bridge across the Tigris which could be opened to allow the passage of shipping and afforded the quick transfer of troops from one bank to the other. Kurna was now some village of importance as we were in a well-fortified position which commanded the approach of all shipping on the two rivers.

One morning we had to dismantle our light and rush it across the river. The Oxfords were having trouble with little bands of snipers, and several Oxford soldiers had received wounds in the camp, so away we went over the bridge, and by sundown, we had our outfit in working order. We then came under the orders of the officer commanding that side of the river. We had orders not to put the light on until the snipers appeared as we wanted to give them a little surprise. A bit of excitement prevailed amongst the troops: They were fresh in the country, having been rushed up to their present position and as yet hadn't fired a round of ammunition on active service.

Nothing unusual happened until the third night; all was quiet up to midnight and pitch dark. Then about one o'clock there was a *bang bang bang*. Within a few seconds we had the engine going and the light playing over the desert. At first we could see nothing until we focused the light to about 200 yards from our position, and there we found the enemy, some 200 to 300. They glared into the light as if they were struck dumb as we traversed the light across their front. They turned and fled in all directions. The Oxfords opened up a rapid fire and must have given them a hell of a time.

Next morning we counted over 50 dead; the wounded must have gotten away. They were all Arabs, not a Turkish soldier amongst them. The commander came round, inspected our outfit, and congratulated us on the splendid assistance we had rendered him. He said he'd report the matter to headquarters. In fact, he was so pleased that I believe if our faces had been a little smoother, he'd have kissed us. Anyhow, the raiding parties stopped.

The searchlight outfit of ours was only a kind of get-together sort of an arrangement which could be dismantled and assembled again in a very short time. It consisted of a Thorny-croft petrol engine of the twin cylinder type, coupled up to a 250-volt generator, with cables leading from the generator to the lamp that burned carbon sticks. A water tank holding about 200 gallons was used for the cooling system. The whole outfit was mounted on an iron base and weighed about 500 pounds. There you were, a contraption which could scare more Arabs than a couple of batteries of artillery. We would open the "picture show" every night more for the troops than out of necessity. They loved to watch the desert through the beam of a searchlight in the expectation of seeing something unusual.

During that lull, the time began to drag and get kind of monotonous for us. We spent much of our time going to Kurna, buying up things to eat, and then practicing our cooking abilities. It was wonderful what a soldier could do out in the field. Give him a couple of pots and a fire, and some of the chefs of Paris would envy him. The dishes which were made had their own special names but are unprintable. The first duty of a soldier is obedience, but ask "Tommy Adkins"; he'll tell you his first duty is his stomach. Then there was washing to be attended to. Laying it out in trenches was a lousy job, but if not taken care of, clothes very soon began to walk away. Our washing was an easy matter. All we had to do was to open a drum of petrol, dip the shirt in and out again, and presto, it was ready to wear.

One day Lord Willingdon from India was on a visit to the Mesopotamian front, and of course we had to get onto the banks and give him a rousing reception as he passed on board the river steamer. He could be plainly seen in the prow of the ship as he acknowledged our cheers.

Gurmit Ali

Our captain paid us a visit with orders for us to pack up at once, get our outfit aboard ship, and proceed to Gurmit Ali, which was a way back down the Shatt-al-Arab about three miles above Basra. That was good news for us as our presence didn't seem to be required any longer where we were. The captain told us that a large Turkish force was gathering at a place called Shabia, a few miles northeast of Basra, and that their object was to recapture Basra and drive the British into the Shatt-al-Arab. He said that Gurmit Ali was the outlet for a small tributary of the Euphrates River which flowed through Hammer Lake, a shallow stretch of water some three or four miles in area. The Turks had a large camp on the lake bank and were reinforced daily by troops coming down the Euphrates.

"Now," the captain said, "what we're going to do is this: We're going to Gurmit Ali and pick up a flat-bottom lighter, which is mounted with two six-inch guns, and proceed to Hammer Lake and see what we can do."

We said "so long" to the Norfolks and Oxfords and set off on our journey. At Gurmit Ali we got coupled up to the lighter, commanded by an artillery major, and proceeded on our way to the lake a few miles ahead. Besides ourselves, we had a firing party of about 50 rank. Arriving in the lake, we could plainly see the large Turkish camp from our port side, and no doubt they could see us, for we had no sooner gotten into the lake when they opened fire with their guns. Their shells fell short, for we were a long way out of their range. On account of the shallowness of the lake, we had to move very cautiously to avoid going aground. We had a small boat, and with it we could circle about, sounding the depth of the water, before we dared venture far ahead with the lighter. The artillery officer wanted to get close enough in to enable him to give the enemy a good peppering and then withdraw out of range, but the depth of the water caused us some anxiety. It varied so much; some places it was only a few inches deep, others a few feet. For two days we manoeuvred about, sometimes getting stuck. Several times all hands had to get into the lake and do what we could to get her afloat. At one time the Turks, seeing our difficulty, opened up on us, their shells falling short by a few hundred yards. We used our light at night to look around and guard against any surprise.

That night the major decided to bombard the camp, so after it was dark, we crept up as far as we dare go and then for about an hour the gunners were busy. We put the light on and could see our shells bursting over the Turks' camp which was all in confusion. Then it was discovered that we were stuck in the mud. We worked all night in the water, but we couldn't budge the ship. At daybreak we were still in the same position. The major got furious.

"Try this, try that," he yelled. He himself got into the water. The Turks got wind of the situation and started to pepper us with shrapnel. We could see their camp had been broken and that they'd partly retired. It was then discovered that the lighter was afloat, so the major ordered the ropes cut which bound her to the ship, and we gradually pushed her out of range and stood by for a time. The Turks had now brought their guns up and were knocking the hell out of our ship. The major decided there was nothing we could do but to continue to push the barge along. When we got into deeper water, we used long poles and gradually found our way back to Gurmit Ali.

The major didn't bother much as long as he got his guns away. He said it might have turned out a lot worse if we had got captured. I think we were all kind of scared for a while. Our searchlight was gone. What were we going to do now? We had no rifles, no equipment; all had been left on the ship. All we had on was a pair of shorts and a shirt; some of the men had no shirts. At Gurmit Ali, a native regiment was on duty. The officers fixed us up with some food while we rested. The next day a motor launch arrived with clothes and took us back to Basra, none the worse for our experience.

Basra was looking much better than when we had left, but it was still being cleaned up. More native troops had arrived; labour battalions had been organized from Egypt and India. They were hard at work, building new roads and improving the waterfront. Docks were in the making, three or four ocean-going liners were laying in the Shatt-al-Arab, field hospitals had sprung up. Drinking stations had been erected where the troops could obtain pure drinking water. Small ice plants were built where ice blocks could be purchased for a few cents. Indian merchants had arrived and had opened small business places. A YMCA party from America had brought lots of canned provisions. The leading stores had been permitted to sell beer and spirits. Beautiful little gardens had been made where the troops could drink tea and coffee or a bottle of ice-cold beer, which was indeed a luxury for a place like thirsty Basra. The supply and transport corps had taken over the rationing of the troops, and everything appeared to be in A-1 order.

Kurna had been evacuated except for a handful of men, the troops having returned to Basra in preparation for the forthcoming battle of Shabia. I received orders to return to my regiment, which was back

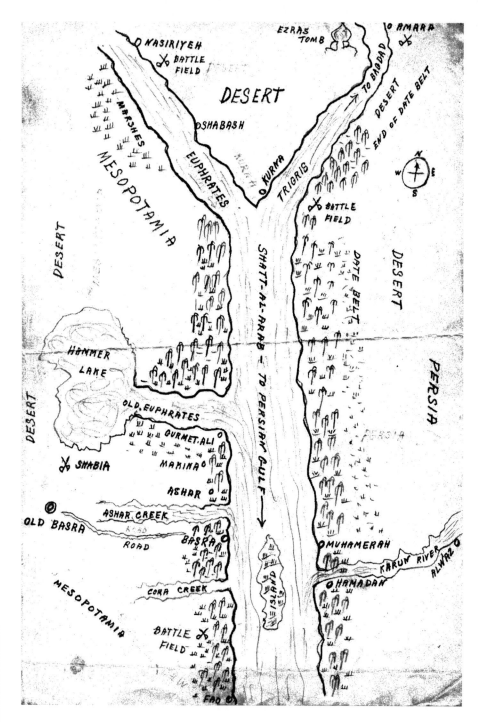

again in the old Turkish barracks, preparing to move off to Shabia. I reported myself to the adjutant, who said something about not expecting me back. "But now you're here, so report yourself to the orderly sergeant." As I walked into the barrack room, my pals gave me a rousing cheer, told me they were going into action again and couldn't do without me, so they'd been obliged to send for me, etc. They were trying to get my goat, so I just said, "dumb liars."

They told me a large Turkish force was waiting to beat hell out of us about 15 miles west of Basra and that every man was to take part in the affair. The regiment was under orders to move at a moment's notice. My pals seemed surprised when I told them they were just a little bit late with their information as I'd already made the acquaintance of the Turks at Shabia on Hammer Lake. And just to cheer them up a bit, I told them that the Turks had some mighty big guns and that we stood a very good chance of finishing the fight in the Shatt-al-Arab. However, the gods decreed that I wasn't to take part in that engagement. The orderly sergeant came to me the next morning and told me to pack up and report myself to the commander of the Royal Indian Marine General Headquarters.

"What for?" I inquired.

He could tell me nothing except that a telephone call had been received mentioning my name and stating that I was to report myself immediately. I was even supplied with transport for my kit and blankets, and very soon I was at GHQ, hunting up the commander of the Royal Indian Marine (RIM). The RIM was a new force which had arrived from India to take over the responsibilities of handling all the marine work and apparently were at a loss for trained men. The commander, a big burly-featured man around 50, was seated at a desk when I entered his office. He nodded and told me to sit down. He was busy writing and on his desk had a large map which he seemed very interested in. After a few minutes, he leaned back in his chair and looked at me.

"I understand that you're a qualified engineer and thoroughly acquainted with oil and gas engines of the marine type."

I stood up and was about to dispute that point when he waved me down and then went on.

"We've got several small tugs and shallow-draught river craft on their way out here, and just now we're badly in need of responsible men to put in charge. Do you think you could handle and manage a native crew?"

"I know," he said, "that you're familiar with the ways and habits of the natives. That," he said, "in itself is half the battle."

I looked at him and wondered where he had got his information from.

"Never mind," he said. "I know what you're thinking about, but I haven't much time." He called a native sailor and told him in Industani to pour him out a whiskey and soda.

"But Sir," I said. "Pardon me, I think you're on the wrong track; you've been misinformed. I know nothing of boats or marine engines. I'm a soldier. I've had no experience in navigation either on sea or rivers and have no papers."

"Tut-tut tut-tut," he said as he stood up. "Papers be damned," he roared at me. "Do you realize this is active service, and I want you to understand that when I say a man is capable of taking a position that I appoint him to, he's already qualified, papers or no papers. Do you understand that?" He helped himself to another drink.

"Yes Sir," I said. "I think I understand now, and you may rely upon me to do my duty to the best of my ability."

"There, there, now you're talking; that's what I like to hear. You'll find accommodations a few yards from the water at the back of this building. Report yourself in the office downstairs. They will fit you out with whatever you require. From now on you'll be on the rolls of the RIM. Now, before you go, I want to give you a word of advice. Don't indulge too freely in this stuff," jerking his thumb towards the bottle of whiskey. "That is all."

I saluted him and walked out, feeling half-paralyzed with fright and visions of ocean liners everywhere. I could hardly believe I was awake. It must be all a dream. There I was, just an ordinary soldier, and in less than half an hour transformed into a sailor and was qualified to take command of the largest river craft afloat. They do some queer things in war time.

At the office, they took down a few particulars, handed me a new playbook, and advanced me 100 rupees which I thought was a fairly good start. I found my quarters to be a little reed hut about 10 feet square and 12 high. I was to report at the office once a day for my orders. My first action was to make out a payment ration slip for one case of beer, signed my name, and put *Capt. RIM* behind it. I gave the slip to one of the native sailors to deliver. He came back, accompanied by a big brawny Arab who had my case of beer on his back. The beer was warm, so I put a few bottles in a sack attached with a string and sunk them in the river to cool off. The next day I was reinforced with some pals who like myself had been transferred to the Navy. For a few days we did nothing but drink beer.

On reporting one morning at the office, I received my sailing orders. I was told I should find steam launch No. 12 lying off a certain jetty. The native crew, including me, numbered seven: one serang, the engineer, and four deck hands. My cargo consisted of cases of food and stores for Kurna. My duties were a matter of appearance only, yet I was really responsible. The serang would take care of the ship and the crew. All I had to do on arrival at Kurna was to report to the RIM officer. I found my ship lying off in the stream, *No. 12* painted in large letters on the bows. "Yo ho!" I sang out. "Yo ho, No. 12!" In a few seconds, a little boat manned by a couple of the crew came to fetch me, and I was soon on board. I was greeted by the serang with "Salaam, sahib. You come, sahib, to take charge of ship."

"You guessed right, serang," I said. "Are you all ready to start?"

"Only waiting your orders, sahib."

Two of the crew hauled up the anchor, and off we went. For a while we stood side by side at the steering wheel; then the serang let me have it. And I amused myself learning to steer the ship which I found was quite a simple job. I was soon master of the steering apparatus. The serang laughed and said "Teak-hai, sahib, teak-hai." He could also speak fairly good English. He told me he lived in Calcutta and was employed on the river steamers and had been a serang a number of years. I asked him why he came to Mesopotamia.

"More rupee, sahib, lot more rupee," he said. "Lots of ships come from the rivers in India to Mesopotamia, not much work for sailor man in India."

I asked him if he was married. "Ah, sahib, me plenty marry. Plenty picininny."

I asked him what he was going to do without his wife.

He grinned, "Um, plenty bib-bee, sahib, in Basra. Arab bib-bee, teak-hai."

The crew members passed the time knocking up their curry and cooking their meals. They had a large flat stone on deck and with another stone they would pound up into a pulp chilies, onions, garlic, and a mixture of other Indian spices. The pulp they would mix with finely chopped mutton and boil which was then dumped on a large bowl of cooked rice. They would all sit around the bowl and have their meal, dipping in with their fingers.

Nothing unusual happened on that trip, and in due course we arrived at Kurna. I reported to the RIM officer; he put a gang of Arabs to work unloading the ship, standing by all the time.

"Have to watch these fellows," he said. "They're like slippery snakes; they imagine everything they see belongs to them. Damn good workers, though."

He gave me some refreshments and told me I could leave for the return trip at my leisure, but as it was a full moon, he advised me to leave at dusk as it would be more comfortable travelling. I had about three hours to spare, so I strolled around and visited my old pals of the search-light section who still had their one light. The British units had left for Basra, and there remained only a few native troops and the artillery which was mostly interested in the enemy's force at Shabia because if the Turks recaptured Basra, our remaining troop artillery would be completely cut off. I told them all I knew which wasn't much. They had a little wireless set and were in constant communication with Basra. I left them in not too cheerful a mood.

The moon was well up when we left, and everybody was in the best of spirits. It was a lovely trip going down the Shatt-al-Arab. A cool, invigorating breeze was blowing; everywhere was dead quiet. The only sound was the *thub thub* of the engine and the sound of the water as it was churned up by the propeller. The moon shone as only a full moon could in the East. Every few minutes we could see a lonely Arab poling his bellem along near the banks. Every now and then a big fish would leap out of the water. The date palms stood out majestically on the banks as I'd never noticed before. The scene was more like watching some magic lantern. Having the tide and current with us, the journey was over all too soon, and before we were aware of it, we were back again in Basra, having completed the 80 miles in a little over five hours.

My regiment had left for the front. A few fresh troops had arrived and were being rushed off. There appeared to be a lot more shipping in the river. Very few soldiers were to be seen. Basra was practically skinned of troops.

The next day all movement was canceled; work was suspended. Orders were issued that all soldiers, regardless of their occupations, which included me, were to stand and be prepared to leave for the front. Reports were coming in that the fierce battle for Basra was in progress. During the day we could hear the faint *boom boom* of the guns over the desert. The battle raged all that day and night. The Turks were putting up a stubborn resistance, and for a time it appeared very doubtful what our position would be. All that night we stood by, but no new orders came for us. I don't suppose we numbered 200 all told. Next morning the climax came. We had the good news that most of the Turks had surrendered; the rest were fleeing northward toward the Euphrates where they had a number of river ships. The population of Basra seemed to be pleased with the result; they had a kind of celebration and decorated the place up with all kinds of flags and bunting. Maybe they had had enough of Turkish rule.

In a couple of days the remnants of our battle army returned to Basra in a pretty bad shape. They told me that it had looked bad for a long time.

We had lost heavily in killed and wounded. Several officers, including the senior major, had been killed, also our regiment sergeant major. My pal Peter had been riddled with bullets and wasn't expected to live. There had been several acts of conspicuous bravery. One of my friends of the searchlight section had been recommended for the Distinguished Conduct Medal. It was reported that the Turkish commander Nur-un-din had committed suicide. Our soldiers had brought back souvenirs: Some had Turkish field glasses, revolvers, gold and silver Turkish coins, and little whips which the Turkish officers used to whip their men into action. All the wounded were placed on board ships and returned to India. It was many a long day before I saw Peter again. He didn't die, but he got badly cut up and lost both his testicles.

Reinforcements now began to pour in from India. Territorials which had been sent out to India to replace the regular troops were now coming out to Mesopotamia. Most of them were mere lads still in their teens. A few airplanes had arrived; motor launches and other river craft were daily putting in an appearance. General Sir Charles Townsend had taken over command of operations in the field, with the intention of pushing on to Baghdad. Headquarters still remained at Basra.

Nasiriyeh

My next adventure was with Major General Gorringe and the capture of Nasiriyeh, a town or city on the Euphrates River about 100 miles from Kurna. I'd been selected to take charge of two motor launches which were to be for the exclusive use of the general and his staff. The motor launches were absolutely new, having just come from England. They were built of wood and were fitted with four-cylinder Kelvin engines. I was ordered to take over these boats and was now under the orders of the general's ADC, and under no circumstances was I to take orders from any other officer.

The boats were numbered 1 and 2 and varied in size. Not being much of a sailor, I called them large and small: The small boat No. 2 could be manoeuvred about in a few inches of water while No.1 required about two feet. They were two pretty-looking boats fitted with brass rods to which were attached awnings to keep the sun off. But the bumps and knocks which we often got soon disposed of those awnings. Three more men from the 1/4th Hampshire Right, a territorial unit, reported to me for duty in those boats. The men were chauffeurs in civilian life, and on account of their background, they had been chosen to drive the boats, one to drive, the other to steer.

We were about two weeks preparing for the expedition. The general had an old Arab mahaila fitted out for his accommodations, another one for the horses. Latrines had to be made on the iron barges which were to accommodate the troops. Those barges were made fast, one on each side of the river steamer. Behind the barges were tied the dhows, loaded with stores, and then the motor launches and other small craft.

The day arrived, and we moved off in three separate processions for Nasiriyeh, looking like a traveling circus. What a game those war stunts were. Our expedition consisted of two British regiments, the 1/4th Hampshire and the West Kents, a regular battalion from India, about three native regiments, and about a half dozen guns. One ship was fitted with a small wireless set. Included in our motor launch equipment was a little primer store outfit with little steamers, pots, and pans. They were very useful to us as we could always make our tea and do our cooking in the boats, which enabled us to be entirely independent because during moves on the rivers, space was so limited that it was next to impossible to get near the galley fires to cook anything. Imagine about 1,000 soldiers trying to get 'round one little galley fire to make hot water, swearing and cussing and fighting. Many were sensible enough not to bother about cooking. The same thing applied to the latrines. All day long, soldiers would wait in line for the privilege. Just before getting dark, the boats would make fast to the banks for the night; then the men could go ashore and do their business. The barges were so densely packed with troops that one false step and into the river a man would be with very little chance of saving himself unless he happened to be an extraordinary strong swimmer. A nonswimmer stood no earthly chance in the swift-flowing, treacherous rivers of Mesopotamia. Needless to say, many a life was lost in that way.

On account of our load and our going against the stream, progress was very slow. The second night we anchored at Kurna. Next morning at daybreak, we were off again. The garrison turned out and gave us a rousing cheer as we entered the mouth of the Euphrates. A few miles up, we passed the village of Shabash on the left bank where a large, fierce-looking tribe of Arabs was encamped. The children were running along the banks stark naked, holding out their hands for baksheesh. The British sloop *Cleo* was stationed there, armed with four- and six-inch guns. As we approached, she let off a few blank rounds in a kind of salute. The village had a shore a mile in length, and there must have been some thousands of Arabs encamped there. They seemed to watch us very gingerly as we passed, but they displayed no arms of any description. At that point, the Euphrates ran into a part of Hammer Lake and was supposed to have a navigation channel for ships to pass through, but that was where our troubles began. Lieutenant Kynah of the RIM and I spent two days sounding the lake for the channel. We could find no more than 12 feet of water and that depth only at different angles; apparently, the lake was covered with sandbanks. I could have told them that before we started, but who was I to volunteer information? Just Private "Tommy Adkins," a mere nobody.

We monkeyed around for a few days. We had to get to the other side somehow but how? No sooner was one ship free than another was stuck. The barges were let adrift, and the troops were ordered into the water to lighten the ship and use their manpower. We wirelessed to Kurna and Basra for assistance, but none was forthcoming. There we were halfway across the lake, and we could neither go ahead nor return. We were in a hell of a pickle. And to make matters worse, the Arabs or Turks, knowing of our plight, began sniping at us every night from some point on the lake or shore. We had no searchlight with us just because we needed one. I mentioned the problem to the ADC, and he must have spoken to the general because a light, all mounted on a shallow craft ready for operating, was rushed up from Basra next day. That night the sniping started again: *pom pom pom pom pom*. We switched our light on, and there they were, a small motor launch with a few Turkish soldiers in it and what looked like a small gun in the bow. The light must have scared them, for they soon disappeared. A few of the sailors from the *Cleo* steamed up in their launch to see if they could render assistance, and the matter was left entirely in their hands. The senior naval officer got to work and ordered the ships to be unloaded and the stores placed in the dhows. He sent to Kurna for more dhows, and by those means, the stores were pushed and pulled into deeper water. When unloaded, the ships could just manage to get along, bumping the bottom all the time. The barges were flat bottom and were easily manoeuvred with a little elbow grease, but we'd lost quite a lot of time, and the general was anxious to go on, but we found our troubles weren't yet over.

Arriving in the river, we found our progress barred by a huge bund that the Turks had built across the river so the water was flowing over both sides of the bund onto the desert which accounted for most of our trouble. I took the general and a few officers to examine the bund. They got up on top and were walking about when all of a sudden *pom pom pom pom*. The Turks were dropping their little one-pounders all around us. The party clambered into the launch and we got away in double-quick time. As luck would have it, none of us were hit. We sent a few rounds from our 18-pounders up the river to scare them off, but they were already gone.

We were delayed again. Before we could advance, that great bund had to be removed. Then it was discovered that we had no explosives. A few shells were discharged into it with little or no effect. Back to Basra again, the wireless was busy, calling for engineers and explosives. During the lull, the Arabs and troops were busy catching fish; they didn't care a damn if we never went on. Finally the bund was blown away sufficiently to allow us to pass.

Then the general had a notion that the river might be mined, so he ordered the two motor launches to proceed in front with a wire hawser stretched the breadth of the river. To say I was feeling shaky would be putting it mildly. I expected every moment to be blown to kingdom come. Just a little bump, and up I'd go. Every now and then the wire would appear out of the water, and someone would yell, "Keep the wire under the water!" I felt like telling them to go to hell or come and do the job themselves. Anyhow, we didn't come across any mines, so our job was abandoned. For three days we advanced up the river without being molested in any way, but on the fourth day, we suddenly came under shellfire. The enemy position couldn't very well be located because both banks were thickly covered with date palms. The general ordered the troops to land on both banks and to stand by, ready to make an advance at daybreak. All night the Turks continued to send shells over, doing a little damage to some of the dhows. The troops got into action the next morning and drove the enemy off after about an hour fighting, leaving two guns behind them which had been mounted at the bend of the river. Apparently the enemy was only a very small force as they showed very little resistance. Two or three of our fellows had been wounded. I was standing on the bank when a bullet whistled past my ear near enough to cause me to take cover behind a tree. The troops embarked again, and we proceeded on our way, lead by a steamer which had two 18-pounders and machine guns mounted on her decks. We camped for the night after we'd passed a small Arab village.

The next morning the staff colonel sent for me and told me to have the small launch ready. He said, "We're going up one of the side creeks for a few miles to do a little reconnaissance work." We were going to take in tow an armed escort of native troops in a bellam.

"Here," he said, "take this," and he presented me with some chocolate bars and a couple of cans of milk. Then my party got into the launch consisting of a machine gun party, who fixed their gun in the front of the boat ready for action. Five staff captains, a native Yemen, and an Arab interpreter. We tied the bellam to the stern of the launch and proceeded on our way up the creek. About a mile or so up the creek, we passed several Arabs who were all armed with rifles. The interpreter would sing out something in Arabic, and we were allowed to pass on until at last we were forced to stop. Some 500 Arabs sprang out and barred our way. I never saw such a rough, murderous-looking crowd in all my life. Every man amongst them was over six feet tall and armed with rifles and horrible-looking swords. It was very easy to see they were on the warpath. My old sergeant's words came back to me: "Remember," he'd said, "if you ever find yourself in a tight corner, save the last round for yourself." I don't mind admitting I was feeling a trifle pale; even their language would frighten an ordinary person. The officers and interpreter got out, but the soldiers remained in the bellam which didn't suit the Arabs, who made the soldiers get out and place their rifles on the ground. My mate, whose name was Nobby Blark, remained in the launch. Our rifles were hidden away under the seat out of sight where we always kept them with our equipment. The interpreter and the chief were jabbering away in Arabic, not a word of which I could understand. I looked around and could see that there was no possible way of escape. One of the officers produced what looked like a roll of Indian rupee notes and handed them to the chief, who went on arguing. Every now and then the chief would point to the launch, and I wondered what it was all about. After a while, myself, the two staff officers, the interpreter, and two Arabs got in the launch and went back to our ship, leaving the eight native soldiers with the Arabs. One of the officers told me on the way back that the Arabs wanted to hold us and the motor launch as prisoners. He said they were a large and powerful tribe and were being brought over on our side. They were suspicious of the paper money and demanded silver.

The party went aboard one of the ships, and I was ordered to stand by with the launch. "Did you think we was ever going to get back, Corporal?" Nobby said to me.

"It looked damn funny to me for a while," I answered. "I certainly don't like the look of them, but I suppose we shall have to take them back." Nobby was an old sailor and had served in the British Navy and on the China stations at Shanghai and Hong Kong and said he'd rather fall into the hands of the Chinks than those murderous-looking Arabs. In about an hour the party was ready. The Arabs appeared with a wooden box, still arguing fiercely with each other. I took them back to the same place and after some more arguing, we were all allowed to depart. Apparently, the Arabs had been bought over and were now on friendly terms with us.

Arriving back once more, I saw the colonel who had given me the chocolate. He smiled and said, "I see you're back all right, Corporal. How did you like the trip?"

"Very good, Sir," I replied, "but I didn't like the look of things for a time. I thought we were never going to get back."

"Rum-looking customers, some of those Arabs, but if you treat them right, they're not so bad. Help us a lot, you know," he said.

We pushed on up the river a few more miles and came to a clearing. There it was decided we should halt. The troops landed on both banks and were ordered to entrench themselves. Small P tents and stores were taken ashore for the general staff. I was lying alongside of the dhow that carried the stores when the orderly who was in charge slipped a case over the side to me.

"Here," he said. "Take this. See what's inside."

On opening the case, I found it contained 12 bottles of Scotch whiskey.

"Gee whiz, what am I going to do with this lot?" I thought. Twelve bottles of whiskey bearing the label of the Army and Navy stores in Bombay and ten years old. It was the general's, and God help me if the case was found in my launch. I'd got it opened up and couldn't return it. I thought about dumping it into the river.

"What shall we do with it, Nobby?" I said to my pal.

"This is sure to be missed," Nobby said. "Knock the top off one, and let's have a drink. That's what I'm badly in need of. Old Gorringe is no more entitled to this than we are. Possession is nine tenths the law," he said. "Besides, how are we to know it belongs to the blooming general? To hell with him. Go on, open up."

What I expected wasn't long in coming. The ADC had checked on the stores, discovered the case of whiskey was absent, and of course reported the matter to the general. Well, his orders were, "That whiskey has got to be found." Then his police and part of his staff were sent 'round the camp, searching for the case, and it soon became known that the general had lost a case of whiskey. That knowledge soon became a kind of a password: "Who pinched the general's whiskey?" We had by then unpacked the bottles and had placed them in different places in the launch: Some we placed in the locker, in the stores of the boat, and under the floorboards. Nobby was continually sucking at a bottle, and I urged him to be careful until the noise had blown over. Everybody seemed to be walking around searching. The provost captain paid us a visit, looked around, but said nothing. I was beginning to get nervous; it seemed as if the search was never going to end. After dark, some of the staff sergeants came to the launch and must have smelled a rat.

"Come on, Corporal. What about a little drop? There's no one about now." Nobby, by this time, was feeling rather generous. He said, "Give 'em a few bottles." Thinking it would be a good thing, I handed over half a dozen and was glad to see them out of the launch. Two more bottles I dispensed by quietly dropping them over the side, keeping two bottles for ourselves. Those I hid away under the floorboards. All next day, the search continued, and many times I had a notion to throw the remaining bottles over the side. I wanted to lose them, and yet I wanted to keep them. Well, it finally wound up by the poor orderly taking the blunt. He was relieved of his job and was ordered back to Basra by the first available boat to rejoin his regiment. But still the password went 'round for days: "Who pinched the general's whiskey?"

Getting back to the war, we were then being visited by a British airplane which would drop messages and then return to Basra as there were no satisfactory facilities for landing. We were waiting for more reinforcement before moving on. Amongst the reinforcement was my old regiment, the Norfolk, or what remained of 'em.

Our force now proceeded on its way up the Euphrates towards Nasiriyeh some 20 miles ahead. By the second day, we had approached as near as we dare go to the enemy's position, a few miles south of the city. The troops disembarked and took up positions on the left bank in preparation for the forthcoming offensive. We had now an officer who had just recently joined the general's staff; he was known as Political Wilson. He was a big, burly, tough-looking man over six feet and looked very smart in his uniform and Sam Browne belt. He wore white tabs on his collar and held the rank of a major. What he was before the war, I don't know, but he could speak Arabic as fluently as any Arab. And when he was dressed up in Arab costume, he looked every inch the part. At night, he'd go away, dressed up in his rig and return again in the mornings. I noticed that he was very often in conversation with the general. For days he'd be dressed as an Arab; then he'd suddenly change into the lady-killing uniform of a natty staff officer. He was free and easy and was permitted to go wherever he pleased. Sometimes on his return journeys, he'd be accompanied by another Arab. I'd seen him sit facing an Arab and every few seconds kick him several times in the shins until the Arab hollered for mercy. I suppose Wilson was trying to get some kind of information out of him, and Wilson knew the right way to do it. He surely had no affection for the Arabs. I had one little experience with him which I'll relate as I come to it.

There I was, kept busy running 'round in the launches, delivering messages, presenting the general's compliments to colonels, and asking if they would please accompany me back to the general's ship for an interview. Sometimes I was gone all day, trying to find a certain officer. Sometimes I'd be taking some staff officer around when the general himself required the launch, and he gave me orders that my launch was to be kept at his disposal at all times. That particular part of the Euphrates was covered with a lot of weed which caused us a lot of trouble with our water circulating system. Sometimes the weed would clog the propeller and stop the engine. On those occasions, I had to lean over the stern of the boat, with somebody holding my legs, and cut the weed away. Many times we had to take a water system apart to clear the stoppage, and it was very seldom that more than one launch was in commission on account of the weed trouble. The intense heat was also causing the seams of the woodwork to open up just above the water line, causing the water to pour in when we had a load and keeping us busy, pumping out all the time.

At all times the officers were very good to us, especially those belonging to the native regiments, and very often after we'd delivered them back to their units, they would give us some little thing: It might be candy or cake and perhaps a bottle of beer. Even the old general himself would send us little tidbits. He had quite a large staff: There was a special guard, about a dozen native soldiers, his police, an Indian cook, a groom and an orderly to look after his stores, besides his clerks and personal staff of officers. Every morning about seven o'clock, I had to take the general across the river for his morning visit to the trenches and then wait for him to come back. One morning when he returned, he thought I'd moved the launch farther up the river, so he asked me who had told me to move. I looked at him, wondering for a moment what he was getting at, so I said, "Pardon me, Sir, I haven't moved. This is where you got out this morning."

He seemed rather doubtful, so he said, "Look, you're right within the range of the enemy's guns." I looked but could see no guns, and then he said, "All right, take me across."

Another morning, a staff officer asked me to take him across the river. "Sorry, Sir, but it's against the general's orders," I told him.

"Oh, come on," he said, "I've got one of my telephone wires broke, and communication is cut off. It won't take a couple of minutes." So I started the engine up and had him very nearly over the other side when someone was hollering at me from the other bank. There stood the general and the ADC, waving their arms and beckoning me to come back.

"Drop me on the bank now; we're so far," said the officer to me.

So I let him off and went to the general.

"Don't you know your orders, Corporal?" he yelled at me. "On whose authority did you take that officer over there?"

I was trying to explain the situation to him when the general broke in.

He said, "If you disobey my orders again, young man, I shall try you by court-martial. Do you understand? Now take me over to the other side."

I said something under my breath. After that, all the officers could go to hell. I made up my mind they wouldn't catch me again. That's what a soldier gets for trying to do his duty. I couldn't quite understand my position. Had I got into his bad books? First he accused me of getting under fire of the enemy's guns, and then he promised me a court-martial, which on active service meant only one thing: the firing squad. I'd have to watch myself very closely in future. Perhaps I didn't realize the seriousness of delaying a general for a few seconds. I was afterwards lectured by the ADC who told me that by disobeying a simple order, I might be the means of sacrificing thousands of lives.

The enemy had begun to trouble us again. Every night, they would bring up a couple of guns and drop a few shells amongst the river craft, making us drop back a few hundred yards. We always slept in the launches. One morning I jumped onto the bank and saw a shell sticking into the ground and was about to pull it out when an officer shouted, "Stop, for God's sake! Don't touch that! It's one of the shells they sent over last night. If you pull that out, you'll probably blow yourself to hell." Later the shell was removed by a long rope, and as it was being pulled out of the ground, it exploded with a roar, leaving a large hole in the ground. I thanked the Lord for being on my side. That was about as near as I ever got to being blown to pieces. The officer had no doubt saved my life.

One night about midnight, I was awakened by Political Wilson. He had an order signed by the general for me to obey Wilson's instructions. He was all dressed up in his Arab costume and had an Arab bellam with him which he made fast to the stern of the launch.

"I want you to take me up the river and drop me on the right bank," he said. "Keep going until I tell you to draw in."

It was a pitch-dark night, and not a sound was to be heard except the *pot pot pot pot* of the motor's exhaust. I knew by a bend in the river that we must be nearing the Turkish lines, but he said it was quite safe and to keep going. Then all at once *whiz bang whiz bang whiz bang whiz whiz whiz whiz bang bang bang bang pom pom pom*. It seemed as if both banks had been turned into hell's fires. Wilson shouted for me to turn and go back as he disappeared with his bellam. In manoeuvring the boat around, I grazed the bank. The propeller picked up a bunch of weeds which stopped the engine. Nobby said, "For chrissake, hurry and cut them bloody weeds away." *Whiz whiz*, the bullets were flying all around us. I hung over the stern while Nobby held my legs. I couldn't cut them weeds away, try as I would.

"Hurry up, Corporal. Jesus, what's the matter? Here, let me have a go." He snatched the knife out of my hand, then yelled, "My God, I'm hit." I could feel the launch filling with water. There was a loud bump as if something had hit the side of the launch. Then I saw a big Arab seize Nobby and pull him over the side; a voice said, "Come on, hurry, be quick!" The Arab pulled me, and I recognized Wilson who had got us into his bellam and was paddling like hell down the river towards our camp and out of the range of the Turks, who were now sending up all kinds of lights showing up the river, but Wilson got us safely back to our camp. Nobby received a flesh wound in the forearm and was treated at the first aid station. Our motor launch had sunk with all our possessions, including our rifles and equipment. All we had was what we stood up in, just a pair of shorts and a shirt. Even our shoes had gone. We never wore our shoes or used our equipment in the boat unless we were expecting any action.

I was ordered to take over the other launch until such time as another one arrived. Nobby was out of action for the time being and was under the doctor's orders. During the morning, I saw Political Wilson, who told me that his scheme had proved a success and that the noise of the motor launch was part of the scheme. His suspicions had been confirmed. He'd discovered that the Turks had several machine guns carefully concealed in camouflaged trenches amongst the rushes on the right bank of the river and were practically invisible to the naked eye.

I thanked him for his timely aid. He had no doubt saved us from a tragic end either from the bullets or possibly from a watery grave. He said he heard our motor stop, and he knew something was wrong; we were only about 100 yards from the concealed trenches. He said both of us had been specially mentioned and expected we would be awarded the Distinguished Conduct Medal. I told him it wasn't the medal that concerned me. I was only too glad to be alive.

Later in the day towards evening, a river steamer with two 18-pounders in the bows crept slowly up the river. I could see plainly that Political

Wilson was on board in his uniform. Very soon we saw his crew open fire, dropping shells all along the right bank, and sure enough the whole bank became alive with fleeing Turks. Our shells must have killed and wounded a considerable number. The Turkish guns returned the fire and our ship had to retire, but we had accomplished what was considered a strategical move.

Everything was now in readiness for the fray which was to decide the future of Nasiriyeh. But unlike other engagements, it was to be a river and land attack; the troops taking part in this adventure were the Hants regiment and the West Kents, two native battalions, and my old regiment, the 2nd Norfolk, which was to be held in reserve. There was six river steamers comprising the *Blosse Lynch*, *Midyedich*, *Shu-shan*, and three T boats. The first three named were the regular Mesopotamian steamers which traded between Basra and Baghdad and were built according to the conditions the rivers called for. They were all fortified with sandbags for protection. On all those steamers, our artillery had been mounted, and each carried a few infantry soldiers.

It was whispered around that the attack was to take place the following morning. I received my orders that night to have the launch ready at a second's notice. About two o'clock, the general appeared with his party, the general himself taking the tiller and steering the launch. It was fairly dark but a beautiful morning; the sky was dotted with millions of stars, and the vision was good. The general steered the launch along the left, so I told the ADC to tell him not to get too near on account of the weeds. He told the general, and he got out into the river. After a little while, he ordered me to stop the engine as he steered alongside the bank; we had just enough way on to reach the bank. As he was getting out, the Turks opened up with rifle fire, the bullets whistling uncomfortably near. The general hurried out of the boat, leaving orders for me to drop back a few hundred yards, get out of range, and await his orders. The fire was so hot it hastened my decision to tie the launch to the banks. I was struck by a bullet in the lower part of my chin. I clambered up the bank and rushed 'round to get behind a mud wall when I was ordered to halt.

"Shoot that bastard!" I heard someone call out. "He's an Arab."

I managed to holler out, "Don't shoot! I'm a soldier and wounded." Two or three of the West Kents came up with their rifles at the ready and with fixed bayonets.

"You nearly got it, pal," they said. "You look just like an Arab in that rig." They bandaged my chin up with the first aid dressing. The bullet had ripped my chin open about an inch, and I had a terrific headache. After a while, the shooting died down, so I got into the launch and dropped back. As I was single handed, I pulled myself along by the bushes, scared that the engine might attract another hail of bullets. In about an hour, the ADC came rushing along and asked me if I was feeling all right. He got in and took the tiller, telling me to start the engine. We returned back to our ships, and he gave orders to advance and open the bombardment. He then clambered aboard the foremost ship and told me to hurry back and pick up the general, who was waiting on the bank. I put the general aboard the ship, and from there, he directed the operations, telling me to follow and keep close by the ship. He had left an officer with me to steer the launch.

Our guns opened with a terrific bombardment of the enemy's trenches, mingled with the rattle of machine and rifle fire of our land forces. For about three hours, we remained in that position, exchanging shells with the enemy. From where I was, nothing could be seen, but I could hear plenty. Several shells were bursting over the ships, and shrapnel was everywhere. The battle raged for another four hours without any progress being made. A staff colonel then beckoned us to get alongside the ship. As we drew alongside, the awning was ripped off our launch by something sticking out. The colonel asked me if I knew the location of the Norfolks and told me to get back to them full speed. My poor old regiment had to get into action with all possible speed. I recognized a few of the boys and waved to them; they looked at me but didn't seem to recognize me, for I had half my face in bandages. We then rushed back to the ships which were now slowly steaming ahead but still keeping up a continuous fire. The *Shu-shan* was listing heavily on one side and looked as if she were about to capsize; she was slowly drifting towards the bank. That was the last I saw of her in that hell. The general was steaming ahead at full speed, his guns still roaring. It was impossible to get the colonel on board, so we hugged the bank. We saw a little opening in the rushes and stopped the launch. The colonel went into a little cave, then came out and called us in.

There were three Turkish soldiers in a sitting position, looking as if they were alive and enjoying themselves, but they were stone dead and had a kind of yellowish look about their features. Their rifles and equipment were brand new. He told me to dump their rifles into the river; their equipment full of ammunition he brought away and put in the launch. The banks of the river were literally lined with these camouflaged trenches. Our ships were still going ahead, blazing away all the time; *boom boom boom bang bang rater tat tat tat* was all that could be heard. We came to a clearing in the date palms and could see the Turks scurrying across the desert in the direction of the Tigris River, and they gradually faded out of sight in the desert mirage. The battle was over. The day had been a hard one for both sides. The Turks had put up a hard fight. They had fought courageously and clean. Both sides had suffered heavily and had endured a 12-hour battle, with Nasiriyeh falling into the hands of the British. The Turks were so tired that they were permitted to rest just where they were, and down they flopped. They had all become mixed up in the last part of the advance. I took the general back to his mahaila, and being about worn out myself, I rolled up on the seat of the motor launch and was soon asleep. The next day the general marched into the city at the head of his troops.

The following days were spent in cleaning up the mess. We collected 24 big guns made by the German firm of Krupps, hundreds of rifles and thousands of rounds of ammunition, stores, and 500 camels. Most of the Turks had fled, leaving their dead and wounded on the field. Our wounded were patched up and sent to Basra; my regiment had embarked and rushed off somewhere.

Our troops camped just out on the outskirts of the city and prepared to settle down. Orders had been issued that there was to be no looting. The general's staff had its camp amongst the date palms. I was provided with a tent near my launch. Nobby had now returned, and together we patched up our awning. For a few days we had it fairly soft.

Nasiriyeh was nothing to boast about, just a few old-fashioned buildings of the usual Eastern pattern which might have been built by Moses. It was a noted resting place for the numerous camel caravans which passed that way. Immediately we occupied the place which was placed out of bounds to all troops on account of the filth and unhealthy conditions which prevailed there. The troops were even forbidden to purchase chickens and eggs.

The surrounding country for some hundreds of yards from the banks was quite fertile, having irrigation channels running from the river, and most any kind of vegetable could be grown to advantage. Watermelons were growing there in abundance. The river was teeming with all kinds of fish, and catching those occupied a lot of our time. One day large numbers of dead fish came floating down the river which continued for a week. It was a puzzle where all those fish were coming from; we were ordered not to eat them.

One Sunday morning, a divine service was held for all English troops. The general himself taking the part of the shy pilot, he had the troops formed up in a three-sided square in front of the tallest building, on top of which a tall flag staff had been erected. Standing by that staff were two British soldiers. After the service had been conducted, a proclamation was read in three different languages: English, Industani, and Arabic. We then sang "God Save the King," the sailors raised the Union Jack to the staff head, and the troops gave three rousing cheers led by the general. A few days later, the general was promoted to the rank of lieutenant general and was knighted. He was now known as Lieutenant General Sir George Gorringe, and when approached by other officers, he was always addressed as Sir George. Sir George was evidently a very religious man; many times I'd seen him in his tent, kneeling by his bed cot, saying his prayers before going to bed. He did the same thing in the morning before breakfast.

He was a tall, stern-faced looking individual. I don't believe I ever saw a smile on his face. He'd rise every morning at daybreak, have a cup of tea, call for his horses and native escort, and make his rounds. He made all the Arabs stand up as he passed. He was very fond of pomp and ceremony. I'd never seen him angry; on the other hand, I never saw him pleased. If he ever was jubilant, he certainly concealed it. He seemed to prefer his own company. Even during his travels on the two rivers, he preferred to shut himself up alone in his Arab mahaila and leave orders that he wasn't to be disturbed unless for some very important military matter. On one occasion while traveling up the Tigris, my motor launch broke loose from the stern of the ship. At the time being aboard the ship, I reported the matter to the ADC who dared not even notify the general. So the ADC had the general's mahaila tied up to the bank while the ship returned to search for my launch. I don't think the general was any the wiser.

It was there that we lost quite a large number of troops through sickness, dysentery, and heatstroke. Men were suddenly stricken and died within a few hours. The intense heat was getting unbearable, very often ranging between 130 and 140 degrees in the shade. I say "the shade" if you could call being underneath the thin cloth of a tent shade. It was more comfortable out in the open sun than under any tent, and only work of a very important nature was attended to between the hours of ten in the morning and five in the afternoon. Many a time I prayed on seeing the sun disappear over the horizon. The nights were not much better; I could lie covered only with a thin garment which allowed me to perspire freely until finally falling off to sleep through sheer exhaustion only to be bitten up by sand flies and mosquitoes. The flies during the day were a pest. Unlike our flies, Mesopotamian flies possessed a needlepoint sting which could cause great suffering. We would sometimes catch those flies, pull their stingers out, and let them go. Some of the soldiers got so weak that when they were attacked with some sickness, they were too weak to fight it off. "Taken sick in the morning, underneath the ground by night" seemed to be the order of the day. That was the cheerful situation at Nasiriyeh in July and August of 1915.

Very often as I lay tossing about, trying to get off to sleep, I'd wonder what use such a country could be to a white man. It was just one big, vast wilderness, full of torment. Industries apart from the dates there were none. The Arabs seemed to be content to lead their own lives and live exactly as they did thousands of years ago. Modern methods and equipment didn't appeal to them; they didn't want them. As long as they could scrape up a meal from day to day, they seemed perfectly happy.

Every precaution was taken by the authorities for the welfare and comfort of the troops. Spine pads were issued as an extra precaution against the sun. Long flaps were attached to a helmet to protect the neck, and dark-coloured glasses were worn to protect the eyes. Lots of those glasses had wires to attach them to the ears. Those wires got so hot that they burnt the ears, so they were all called in and replaced with elastic.

One morning about the end of August, I was issued orders to draw 12 days' rations. The general had received orders to return to Basra, news cheerfully received by us. The time was beginning to drag, for our duties were practically nil, occasionally running across the river with a message to some commanding officer. I made out a ration chit and sent Nobby for the rations. He came back loaded up, sweating from head to feet but smiling all over.

"What's the joke, Nobby?" I asked.

"Wait and see what I've got for you."

He emptied out the rations: tea, sugar, bread, biscuits, onions and bully beef, and a half side of bacon.

"There," he said. "Don't you think I've done good, Corporal?"

"Excellent, Nobby," I said.

Then he grinned. "Wait and see this." He dived his hand in the bag and brought out a bottle.

"What do you think of this, old soldier?" he said. "He's full, rum rations for 12 days, Corporal. Here, have a pull. It's damn good. I had a couple of tots with the S and T sergeant. He's got barrels of it 'round there. Sorry we've got to go away from here," he said.

"I'm not sorry, Nobby. I'm damned glad; this place is making me feel sick."

"Get a good swig of that rum into you. That's the best medicine there is in this damn rotten climate. Why, I used to think that China was bad, but Jesus Christ almighty, I'd sooner be in China a thousand times over than in this hell of a country."

I could tell Nobby had had more than a couple of shots. He kept on jabbering away for about an hour.

"Are you ready to leave, Corporal?" asked the ADC.

"Yes sir," I replied.

"You're to follow the ship as soon as we leave. Have you got plenty of petrol?"

"Plenty, sir," I replied.

"Keep your eyes skinned; we may be off any moment now," he said.

It was after midday when I saw the general get aboard his mahaila. I aroused Nobby, who had fallen off into a doze and was snoring to beat the band. About five minutes after the general got underway, we followed, keeping behind a few hundred yards. I was sitting by the engine, and Nobby was at the tiller. He would, every few minutes, take a pull at the bottle of rum.

We had arrived at a small Arab village named Shuki-Shuk, where the general stopped for the night. There was a small detachment of native troops garrisoned there, part of the line of communications. I'd tied the launch to the stern of the ship and was busy with my pots and pans in the galley, trying to knock out some kinda meal when one of the native crew started hollering in Industani, and he came running to the galley.

"Sahib, sahib," he said, waving his arms frantically. "Juldy, sahib, duc-ra, sahib," pointing to the river. "Um bolo paw-nee nech-i ruh-ho," meaning my pal has fallen into the water. I looked around in amazement and started to holler for Nobby. I rushed up onto the officer's deck and reported what the native had said, and a party of us searched the river for two hours but all in vain. Poor old Nobby was gone forever.

Before leaving the next morning, the general left orders that if the body was recovered, it was to be taken back to Nasiriyeh for burial. Nobby had often told me that he was always scared he'd be drowned. Although he was an old Navy man, he never was able to swim. Amongst his little kit bag, I found his home address in Winchester, England. I wrote to his people and told them the sad news, but I received no answer. I think some of the officers thought that Nobby had had a little booze because the launch was smelling awfully strong of rum, but I didn't think he was drunk because I found quite a half bottle in the locker.

We continued our journey and arrived at the lake. There we were delayed for a couple of days owing to the low water. At first it was decided to leave the launch behind, but the general wouldn't hear of that, so my launch was hoisted up between two dhows and poled across. The general's mahaila was poled across, but the ship had to remain behind. When we got into the river again, I took it in tow and so arrived at Kurna.

Kut

There we found our orders had been canceled. We got news that Generals Sir Charles Townshend and Delamain had taken Amara and were pursuing the Turks, who were retiring towards Kut. A high-speed tug was waiting to convey our party to

Amara where General Gorringe was to take command. So off we went again at full speed, waiting only to get rations. I was to be towed in the stern of the tug and remain in the launch.

Amara was about 200 miles by river from Kurna. The general was in such a hurry, he even traveled at night, a thing he'd never done before. And what a trip. Never shall I forget it. At every bend in the river, my launch would be thrown high and dry on the bank; the next second, I was jerked back to the water again. It was worse than being in a rough sea. I had to hold on for my very life. I stuck it out all through the night; sleep was out of the question. The next day I could stand it no longer, so somehow I managed to climb aboard the tug. The River Tigris had so many bends and corners that sometimes it looked as if I were way back where I started. It also differed in breadth: Some places it was a matter of a few hundred feet, and others it broadened out to a few hundred yards. On account of its swift-flowing nature, all ships proceeding upstream had to make way for ships coming down. In spite of those precautions, many collisions occurred. That night my launch broke loose, and the tug had to steam down the river about five miles before we recovered the launch in one of the bends. I then made it fast to the side of the tug but very nearly came to grief when passing through the narrows. Many times I heard the sides crack as the launch was pushed against the bank.

We eventually arrived at Amara about seven o'clock one morning. The sun was well up in the heavens, giving the city a most beautiful appearance. From a distance, the white clay brick structures appeared to give the impression of a long line of palaces fronted by a wonderful promenade. But as we drew nearer, we found it was only due to the position of the sun playing on the buildings. We drew up to a landing stage, and the general immediately went ashore. I was tired, having had very little sleep during the rough journey, so I lay down in the launch and fell off to sleep.

During the day, the general took over a large building facing the river. There was a large courtyard with little rooms built 'round the square, rooms looking as if they might have been the women's quarters of some sheikh. In one of those I was told to make my home.

Amara differed very little from the other cities of Mesopotamia with the exception that there appeared to be a larger gathering of white Jews who were mostly businessmen. The Arab population, who had not yet become acquainted with the English, took advantage of the little garrison Townshend had left behind, taking to robbery and thieving. The Arabs started by pillaging our rations. Then they got to stealing horses and mules, so the general, after several warnings had been issued, had a gallows erected and the crime of horse stealing became punishable by hanging. Several Arabs were hung before the nuisance was put to a stop.

The short stay there proved a merry-go-round for me. The general would take his morning ride, accompanied by his Punjabi escort, and run all the Arabs down who didn't stand to attention when he passed. Sometimes I'd take him down the river to do a little shooting. On those occasions he'd have about half a company of soldiers to act as beaters, but he very seldom shot anything larger than a little cock sparrow.

Thinking I could do better, I went and bought up about a couple of dozen chickens and a few ducks and kept them in one of the rooms in the courtyard. After about a week, the birds annoyed the general so much that he gave orders to have them destroyed. I sold most of them at a good profit to the staff officers' mess, so no doubt the general enjoyed some of my chickens, though I was hoping at the same time he didn't get a bone in his throat and choke. I was sorry to lose my livestock as I was getting a regular supply of fresh eggs.

I made friends with a young Jew who would come 'round to see me every day to see if I needed any shopping. I'd let him go to the bazaar and purchase anything I might require. Although beer and spirits were practically unobtainable, the young Jew could always keep me well supplied, and many times after dark, he'd bring around a pretty girl and want to leave her with me for the night. Needless to say, being a soldier, I always turned that chance down. There were lots of pretty girls in Amara.

Every day, ships coupled up to barges loaded with troops were passing through Amara on their way to join General Townshend. On 30 September 1915, the news came through that he'd captured Kut, a small village and important military position, and was pursuing the Turks up the Tigris. Our losses there included a couple of airplanes which had failed to return.

About two weeks later, we packed up and were on our way to Kut. On the way we stopped at Sheiks Sa'ad where Townshend had brushed away a small enemy force and had left a small garrison of native soldiers behind. About a week later we steamed into Kut where the historic siege was to take place later. There was nothing very appealing about Kut; except for its most filthy conditions and its strategic position, the only thing of any importance seemed to be a large, ugly-looking scaffold which had been built on the front near the river. That piece of work had been specially erected to hang two Arabs who had been caught mutilating our wounded soldiers as they lay on the battlefield. The Arabs had been caught in the act of cutting out the testicles of British soldiers.

Those two rebels had been tried under military law and sentenced to be hung. The carrying out of the sentence was still pending when General Gorringe arrived, who ordered the execution to take place the following morning. The Arab population was ordered to turn out and witness the ghastly proceedings. When everything was in readiness, one of the prisoners was marched to the foot of the scaffold where he was blindfolded. He was jabbering away in his native tongue something about Allah as he was assisted up the steps by two soldiers. He was then placed over a little trap door and his legs tied together. While that was going on, an Arab interpreter was reading from a paper he held, explaining to the population why the punishment was being inflicted. The noose was then adjusted by a sergeant, and at a signal, about 50 British soldiers pulled on a rope, and down went Mr. Arab to meet his maker. After ten minutes had elapsed, he was pulled up again and exposed to all his pals gathered around. He then disappeared from view to await his partner in crime.

After loafing at Kut for about two weeks, I was wishing something would happen to get us moved from such a desolate hole in the desert, as barren as a rock. Not even the old familiar date palms were to be seen. General Townshend was still making his way towards Baghdad about 100 miles from there. It was 30 November 1915: I was awakened in the morning and told to be prepared to leave at a moment's notice. I was glad to hear the news, quite expecting we were going to move up the Tigris to Baghdad. Every man was ordered to start digging trenches; even the officers were employed at that game. All day we worked hard. Lots of the Arabs were rounded up and put to work. Not a word of information was given as to why all the digging was going on. Were we expecting an attack, I wondered. If so, what good were we, only a handful of men; I don't suppose the whole garrison numbered more than 100.

Just as the sun was going down, I was ordered to my launch, which was being loaded with all kinds of office materials, books, etc., and was told to proceed under my own power back to Amara and await there for further orders. I was given an escort of two of the general's guard. Having a good strong current with me, I arrived at Amara a few hours later to find the city all in an uproar. General Gorringe arrived back at Amara a few hours after my arrival and ordered all the population dispersed. The Arabs were clustered around in groups, talking excitedly, and then I heard the news: At Ctesiphon, General Townshend was surrounded by the large Turkish army under the German General Von der Gotz, and the siege began, which marked the beginning of the end of Indian Expeditionary Force D and the remains of my dear old regiment, the 2nd Norfolk which had left India in November 1914 over 1,000 strong. Not one man who survived the siege and fell into Turkish hands ever returned. It could only be surmised what happened to those poor devils. Only by the skin of my teeth was I saved from a similar fate, and I often wondered what prompted General Gorringe to quit Kut. When I left Kut, there were very little provisions and all that General Townshend found when he came flying for his life with his little army to Kut was an empty cupboard to feed about 20,000 famished troops. Those poor buggers must have been starved for weeks.

General Gorringe at once got busy and collected all the available troops at his command and set off up the Tigris again. But it was only a waste of good energy. His handful of troops was next door to useless against some 100,000 Turks, so he had to await the arrival of more troops from India and England. During that waiting period, the few airplanes we had were used to some advantage chiefly in dropping food into Kut. Ten tons of provisions were dropped by those planes.

One morning General Gorringe was wounded while on his way 'round, taking his usual morning observations, and was rushed back to Amara to have the bullet extracted. He was back again within a few days as active as ever.

The Turks had established themselves at Sannaiyat in a formidable position astride the Tigris about 12 miles northeast of Kut. The situation at the time was of a very despairing nature for the British, and only a miracle could do anything to help relieve the terrible sufferings of Townshend's besieged force. General Gorringe was at his wit's end; he was powerless to attempt an attack which would have ended in the useless slaughter of his men. He was no doubt a soldier from the crown of his hat to the toe of his boot and always had the welfare of his troops at heart. No one could tell what his feelings were for those poor fellows locked up only a matter of miles away in Kut. Yet how was he to get there? What was he to do under the circumstances? Did any general have a greater problem to work out? There was a large Turkish force surrounding Kut under a German command and another large force, which could have swallowed Gorringe like a shark swallowing small fishes, strongly entrenched at Sannaiyat to oppose him.

Well, General Gorringe did attack and as might be expected was repulsed. The afternoon of the attack, I took the general and staff up the river as far as we dare go, landed them on the left bank, and received orders to drop back a few hundred yards and wait for further orders. Before very long, I could hear the battle was in progress by the old familiar sound and occasionally a shell bursting within a few feet from where I was. During the evening, I received a message to retire back to our camp and pick up a medical officer, whom I found standing on the bank, waiting with his kit and field equipment. He told me to take him up to the front. Looking for a convenient place to land, I came abreast of one of the river steamers and drew alongside, holding on to the ship while the doctor was getting ashore carrying part of his equipment. Without any warning, the ship's paddles started to twirl at a terrific speed, drawing the bows of my launch under the water. To save myself, I was forced to jump onto the steamer in total darkness; otherwise, I should have been sucked under the wheels and been crushed. We were well within the range of the enemy's gunfire, and bullets and shrapnel were flying all around us. *Bang bang crack* and over toppled the ship's funnel. I made a mighty jump in the darkness and landed safely on the bank. I came in contact with the medical officer who was all right but had left some of his supplies in the launch. In that predicament, I waited for daybreak to ascertain my position, hoping in the meantime to fall across some of the general staff. I was disappointed.

They were now bringing back some of the wounded and laying them side by side. I think most of them must have been dead because there was never a word or more from them. In my distressed position, I hardly knew what to do. I had no helmet, and the sun would soon be up. My launch was gone; I didn't know where. It had all my belongings in it. I thought it must have sunk. I must admit that I was wishing the war would end. I felt that I was all alone. My boat had gone. I'd lost all my pals. My poor old regiment was gone. Surely I had no business to be alive, yet there I was, all dressed up like a London urchin, walking along the banks of the Tigris with nowhere to go. Had anybody ever been in such a predicament? I resolved to find my way to the nearest RIM officer and report myself.

After walking about six miles I came across some troops disembarking and got aboard one of the ships returning to Basra. I got the captain to take me as far as Amara. There I reported to the RIM officer who was living in a tent. I knew him, having met him at Basra. He took me in and fixed me up good, told me to help myself to a bottle of beer and have something to eat. You bet I did; I was nearly famished. He told me not to worry about the launch as he had got two or three, and I could take which one I wanted. He also gave me several parcels which had arrived from the ladies of India. Those were godsends; they contained shirts, socks, candy, cigarettes, canned goods, etc. So I was pretty well set up again. The next day I got rigged out with some clothes and with my new launch, I attached myself to a steamer going upstream and made my way to headquarters which had dropped back a few miles and was now on the right bank.

Gorringe's attack had proved an utter failure, and nothing could be done until we received reinforcements on a very large scale. It was estimated that the enemy's strength was around 200,000, and the very existence of our men in Kut entirely depended upon what the airplanes could drop them. The whole situation in Mesopotamia had come to a sudden halt and didn't look very rosy for the British, ironically enough at a time, January and February, when the climatic conditions offered their best for the movements of troops. After that, the weather gradually became unbearable. For two months, nothing was done. The troops strongly fortified themselves while large reinforcements were arriving daily. The Turks appeared to be amusing themselves by cleaning up their camps during the lull in operations. Every day, dead camels, horses, and even dead Turkish soldiers would float down the river. Evidently that was their method of disposing of their dead. Many a time I had been getting my drinking water out of the river just as a half-dozen dead Turks floated by with their hindquarters sticking out of the water.

One day there was an exchange of prisoners. Amongst them were a few Turkish women, the wives of officers who'd been unable to quit Basra at the time the British occupied that city in 1914. They were brought to a point just behind our front line in a river steamer, then transferred to my launch and conveyed under a white flag as far as the Turkish lines where I was halted by a barrage of rifle fire and met by a detachment of Turkish officers and men who took over the ladies and escorted them away. I was then permitted to return and bring another load until the move was complete.

That same evening the Turks sent over a succession of shells which were bursting some 500 yards behind our lines, and I wondered what they could be aiming for, as there were no troops anywhere near. The next night about the same time they brought their guns up and started the same game. They repeated that move several times. At last they hit their target. One of our ammunition barges went off with such a loud explosion that it rocked the earth for miles around, and it was some time before I realized what had happened. Strange that the shelling should have started the same day as we handed over those Turkish women.

Another unsuccessful attempt was made by Gorringe in April to relieve Townshend. All hopes for him had now faded away, and so Sir Charles Townshend was forced to surrender on 30 April 1916, having endured the siege for 143 days. His army then numbered 8,000 men out of an original total of 20,000, 4,500 being accounted for during the retirement on Kut, so during the siege, he must have lost 8,000 men from starvation and disease. So ended gallant little Indian Expeditionary Force D.

No further advance was attempted during the next two months. General Sir George Gorringe was recalled to England. I conveyed the unhappy general on his last trip down the Tigris to join his river steamer. As he got out of the launch to climb onto the steamer, he looked at me and said, "Goodbye, Corporal."

I saluted him and said, "Goodbye, Sir."

That was the last I ever saw of him. Many a time I said to myself, "Poor old Gorringe; he did his best against great odds."

He was succeeded by General Sir Stanley Maude. That brilliant general had a short but very successful career during the few months he was in charge of operations. The force had now become known as the Mesopotamia Expeditionary Force. Large reinforcements were now arriving from England. After the fall of Baghdad in March 1917, he accepted the invitation of some Arab sheikhs to attend a conference, and at that meeting it was said he accepted the hospitality of the Arabs by dining with them, and after drinking some milk, he was taken with a violent sickness and died a few hours afterwards. It was rumoured that he had been poisoned, which may or may not have been the case.

About that time I was feeling down in the dumps. My appetite left; I couldn't eat. The sun seemed to have an unbearable effect upon me which was something new to me, and I was continually more or less in a state of fever. The headquarters doctor doped me up with pills and castor oil until I felt I had no intestines left, so under the doctor's advice and backed up with his recommendation, I sent in an application for leave on the grounds of ill health. To my surprise, my request was granted under the general's signature. The document stated that I was to be accorded passage to India and back. A few days later, I presented this document to GHQ at Basra. No red tape or obstacles were placed in my way, thanks to the general's signature. I was granted one month's leave of absence to date from the day of my arrival in India to date of embarkation for returning, giving me one full month in India. I was promoted to the rank of acting sergeant. The promotion, it was pointed out to me, was for the conveyance of securing better accommodations during the voyage, which I greatly appreciated. Upon my return, I was to report at GHQ Basra. I need hardly say that I was feeling "top hole" after nearly two years of being pulled and bumped about in that hell upon earth of a thirsty country. I was badly in need of a change, if only from the mosquitoes and sand flies.

I had to wait at Basra for about a week for a suitable steamer. The time afforded me the opportunity to get rigged up with suitable clothing and to look around and note the improvements which were still in progress. Basra had been transformed into a large shipping port where the large ocean-going liners could dock alongside its newly made wharfs. Large cranes were at work unloading ships. Rolling stock and rails had arrived, and the Basra-Baghdad Railway was well under way. Electric plants had been installed in hospitals and barracks. The British-American firms Lynch Brothers and Gray-Mackenzie Company, Stricth-Scott shipping agents, the Basra Trading Company exporters of dates and grain—all those merchants had rendered the British some valuable service when we first landed in 1914. Most of the river ships had been owned by those firms and were confiscated for the troops. All those firms were doing a large volume of business under the British flag.

All kinds of money exchanged hands in the purchase of goods. Indian rupees, Persian krans, Turkish copper, silver, and gold coins, and English sovereigns could occasionally be seen. The railway which was then being built would enable passengers to travel to Baghdad in a few hours over the desert, whereas the same trip took weeks by river, the old form of transportation. It was the combined efforts of those firms which had created the railway venture. It was those merchants who threw open their warehouses and other buildings to house the British force; to those people we had to give thanks for sending down their steamers to convey us to Basra after our first victory in Mesopotamia, which saved us from a long and tiresome journey across the desert sands.

Basra was 70 miles from the sea and a free port. The great camp at Maclimeh just north of Basra was well under construction, built to accommodate some thousands of troops, and was set amongst the date palms, affording some protection from the sun. A large motorboat dockyard was also being built where all repair work could be carried out under the supervision of the RIM. All that work was progressing with the front line of our fighting forces only about 200 miles away. Nobody knew at the time which way the tide was going to turn; we were taking a huge chance with a small army holding in check some 200,000 fighting Turks under German leadership.

The time for my departure arrived, and in August 1916, I shook the sands of the Arabian desert from my feet as I boarded the B1 steamer for Bombay, thanking my lucky stars I'd been permitted to remain alive. The Arab pilot service was now operating, and we had one on board who took us as far as the sandbar at the mouth of the Shatt-al-Arab. We passed Fao, a small village which used to be the terminal telegraph line connecting the cable to Bushire in Persia and India. As we entered the Persian Gulf, we left Koweit, a town of some 50,000 Arabs commanded by an old sheikh who flew his own flag.

On Leave

The ten-day journey to Bombay was all which could be desired, and I soon made some new chums, all of whom were like myself going on leave. We spent most of our time drinking and indulging in a mild form of gambling with cards. By paying a few rupees, we were given first-class fare. It was arranged among four of us that we'd spend a week together in Bombay before going our different ways. Walter Wainwright, a Eurasian sergeant of the RE, promised to show us all there was to be seen in Bombay. He was a native of Calcutta but had spent several years in Bombay.

Arriving at that city, we had to wait about a couple of hours before we were towed into the docks. It was there that we saw for the first time ships undergoing the camouflaged painting. We immediately landed and were driven to the sailors' home which was to be our headquarters for a few days. It was raining hard. The southwest monsoon was at its height; the weather was stuffy and depressing. But what did that matter to us? We were free and away from military discipline. We acted more like a bunch of kids just let out of school; we laughed and joked at most everything we saw. We had a pocket full of money, and we intended to use it.

We discovered that some of the hotels and saloons had been barred to soldiers and sailors, but that act wasn't out of any disrespect for the forces but more to safeguard their own interests and to protect their property. And a mob of soldiers returned from the front were hardly responsible for their actions when full up with John Barleycorn. One proprietor made the mistake of putting up a sign which read "Sailors and dogs not admitted." His place was stormed one night by the combined forces which ransacked the place, leaving the poor proprietor amongst a pile of wreckage and broken bottles.

Each of us purchased a cheap suit of drill and dressed up in civilian attire, which was more comfortable than the ordinary military uniform although that change was strictly against regulations. We were then prepared to see what Bombay was made of, Walter acting as guide and interpreter. We visited all the best hotels, including Watson's and the well-known Taj Mahal Hotel, dining on the best that those places could produce. At night we done the theatres and other places of amusements which the city had to offer. Queen Victoria must have been greatly honoured by Bombay. There was the great Victoria railway terminal with its magnificent building of native craftsmanship, the Vic docks, the Vic miadan, Vic road, Vic gardens, and the Victoria monument of the Queen in white marble. That monument was the cause of a lot of trouble with the authorities some years before the war. Bombay awoke one morning to find that somebody had painted their beloved god with a coat of black paint, and that act started the uproar. Who had the audacity to do such a thing? Nobody knew, and it went down in history as one of the unsolved crimes of Bombay. We next visited the famous Elephanta Caves and Oyster Rock, which didn't interest us very much, only from a military view, for both places were being mounted with large guns and powerful searchlights. We saw the large Tower of Silence on Malabar Hill where the Parsee took their dead and placed them on a grid where the big vultures devoured their flesh and the bones dropped through the grid to mingle with those of their pals who had gone before.

One morning Walter suggested that we take in the other side of Bombay and see a little of the native quarter. He said we might be interested in a few things that went on behind the scenes. So off we started in a gharry. Walter told the gharry-wallah to drive to Grants Road. On the way, we passed two native funeral processions. The natives were walking four abreast, chanting a tune to the accompaniment of some brass cymbals which they kept clanging together and giving off a hideous noise. Then came the corpse crushed up in a kind of sitting position on a flat-bottom lorry drawn by a couple of bullocks. Behind that came a long stream of mourners, eating bananas and oranges and chewing betal nuts, appearing more like they were having a party. Walter told us they were off to the funeral pyre, where the body was burned on a pile of wood. He said the natives died by the hundreds in Bombay.

Grants Road, I soon found out, was the red-light district of that huge city. On both sides of the street were houses two and three stories high, full of all nationalities of women of all ages from 15 upwards. We dropped in on the ground floor of one of those houses and found ourselves in the company of four buxom wenches, all Europeans. Those girls all had their own private bedrooms where they entertained their men friends. Beers and liquors could be obtained in those places at exorbitant prices. After a few drinks, we left, much to the astonishment and disappointment of the girls, who called after us and shouted something in their own language which we didn't understand. A few doors farther down we were beckoned by some Japanese girls who were looking out of a second-story window. Walter said, "Come on, let's go in here!" as he dived up the stairs. In a large furnished front room, we found half a dozen almond-eyed Japanese damsels perched up on high stools, playing cards 'round a table. As soon as we were seated, they came and planted themselves on our knees and started to smile and whisper sweet nothings in a language which would have been good to know. None of those girls knew a word of English except the girl who appeared to be the boss. She tried to tell us the girls had only been in India a short time, and any of them were available for a rupee; entertainment for all night was five rupees. The girls were all the time pulling our sleeves and making motions toward the bedrooms. Walter had already disappeared with one of the girls. We drank beer and ate nuts and Japanese sweet meats in that establishment while the girls played all kinds of string instruments and sang songs in their native tongue. We left those little butterflies with some baksheesh and promises to return to witness a native cancan dance. There in a large room on a raised platform draped with curtains were six native girls stripped naked and going through all kinds of motions with their shining bodies glistening in the sunlight to the accompaniment of a drum. They finished their dance by forming a straight line facing us, wiggling their whole bodies from head to foot, then falling flat on their faces, salaaming us and asking for baksheesh.

As we moved along the street, we passed locked doors which were guarded by iron rods, and behind those doors could be seen native girls of all ages from about seven years and up. Some of them had powdered their faces with white chalk to make their appearance look more appetizing to the passersby. Those unhappy creatures, Walter told us, could be bought for a mere four annas, about a nickel American money. What a sordid existence to lead. It was hardly believable. How on earth could such a bunch of humanity live, fighting each other for men's favours like a lot of wild beasts?

Leaving this colourful picture behind us, we moved on. Walter was talking to a pretty-looking native woman who, after eyeing us up and down, allowed us to pass on upstairs into a large room and supplied us with whiskey and soda. Walter turned the whiskey down and told her to bring a fresh bottle which hadn't been opened. After a while she conducted us up a narrow stairway to a long passageway which had craftily concealed little peep holes in the wall looking into the rooms beyond. In the first room could be seen a man and a woman lying on a bed in the loving position of sexual communication. In another room could be seen the images of two persons, but their position and what they were doing was impossible to describe, but it was easy to make out that they were of the opposite sex. In the third peephole there was more light, and in there, reposing on an Indian charpoy, could be seen a maiden wearing the clothes she came into the world with. Apparently she was asleep. Stretched out on the floor was her male companion dressed in European clothes. He was fast asleep and no doubt in a drunken slumber. On a little table stood a glass and bottle of whiskey. He might have been a sailor from one of the ships, who knows. There were other peepholes, but I went back to my whiskey and soda, leaving my companions to get on with their amusement for which we had paid one rupee each, including drinks. Out in the street was all hustle and bustle; natives and men in European dress could be seen going and coming from the houses. Little kids about seven or eight years old were soliciting the human trade. One little kid grabbed hold of my hand, saying, "Come, sahib, nice Muhommedan gal."

"Let's go, Walter, and see what this kid's up to."

So we followed the youngster who kept looking back to make sure we were following him. He brought us to a side doorway in an alley. Inside was an old hag of a woman who was grinning all over her face. She made motions for us to wait and disappeared through a doorway. Presently she beckoned us into the room, and there stood five young girls with nothing on. We threw them a few annas and left. Outside, the kid was waiting for his baksheesh, salaaming us all the time. After a while we returned to the little Japanese girls and spent a jolly evening, and so ended our visit to the forbidden haunts of Bombay city.

Our week's celebration having come to an end, we were preparing to go our different ways. Walter was going to his home in Calcutta; the other two were going up to the Punjab in northern India. I'd decided to go to Belgaum and see if any of my old regiment was still in existence and pay a visit to the disbursing office to get reimbursed. But we all promised to be in Bombay again a few days before our sailing date to return to Mesopotamia.

I found Belgaum to be about the dullest place in India. There were only about a couple of dozen men in the barracks, and they were doing police duty and generally taking care of the barracks. A few of the wounded men were walking about in hospital uniform. I remained a few days and then packed up and went to Bangalore, a large military centre in central India. There the absence of troops was keenly felt. All the large barracks were practically empty. I remained there a week, cycling around to the different places of interest, which largely included the hotels and saloons, drinking beer.

Returning again to Bombay a few days before sailing time, I came across my old pal Peter in the dockyard. He spotted me first.

"Hello, Sergeant," he said as he slapped me on the back. "How the hell are yer? I ses yer bin going in fer promotion. How did yer come ter git that way? I thought yer was dead with the rest of them. Come and have a blooming drink! It's quite a treat ter see one of the old regiment. You ought ter see the blooming kids they've bin sending out 'ere. Why, they ain't got the blooming cradle marks out o' their arse yet."

Peter took me to one of the sheds that had been turned into a canteen and bought two pints of beer.

"Do you know we've had a hellova time getting any beer until these last few days. It seems as if they've drank all the beer up in the old country. This stuff is imported from Japan; 'taint much good, but still it's better than water."

"What are you doing 'round here?" I asked him. "Are you going back to Mesopotamia?"

"What, me go back to that vermin-eating hell? Not me, Corporal. I supposed ter be an invalid, but I got a good job here, dodging around with a few messages for the embarkation office. Don't make me laugh, Corporal, asking me to go back to Mesopotamia. Why, din't yer know that they filled me with so many holes at Shabia that I'm nothing but a blooming human sieve? Look here, an' here," as he showed me the scars on his legs and arms. "And the doctors say that I've still got about half a ton of lead inside me somewhere. I'm just hanging out fer this 'ere war to finish, an' then it's home sweet home fer Peter. Now tell us something about yerself. Oh, wait a minit while I git a couple more beers. How would yer like a peg o' whiskey? We got plenty here, and I don't have ter pay only once a week on pay day."

"Let me pay, Peter. I have plenty of money."

"Oh, no, I din't mean that. You don't have ter pay fer nothing; you're my guest as they says while yer here."

I told Peter the old bungalows in Belgaum were all locked up and were in a state of mourning.

"Damn good job, I don't want ter see that damn place, either, bring back too many memories fer me. The only thing I wish now is that I had a job like this in old England, and then I'd be satisfied fer the rest o' my natural life. But honest, Corporal, how much longer do yer think this 'ere war is going to last?"

"I'm sorry, Peter, but it looks to me as if it's hardly started. Neither side seems to be getting very far ahead on the Western Front, and thank

God we never went there. Our front was plenty good enough for us. Supposing Germany wins. What are we going to do then?"

"Haw, yer a cheerful sort of a sojer. They ain't gonna win anyhow. Yer wait till the blooming Yanks get inter this lot; they'll damn soon upset this 'ere blooming shootin' gallery. We had news they was turning out ships by the hundreds."

"Well, Peter, I hope they won't be long; there's plenty of room for them right now. I don't see what you've got to worry about. As far as you're concerned, the war is over."

"Fer blimey, Corporal, you're right there," said Peter. "But that ain't going ter bring all our old pals back. Jesus, them bloody Turks sure did fight at Shabia." Peter got up and went away and came back with two whiskeys. "Here's looking at you, Corporal," he said as he swallowed his at one gulp. "Supposing you and I take a look at Bombay tonight."

"All right, Peter, but not too much booze. Meet you here at eight o'clock sharp."

Peter was there at eight o'clock all right; in fact, he'd been there ever since I left him, still knocking the beers back. "Hullo, Corp-al, think we'll havta put our little trip off. I kinda feel a little bit top-heavy. Come eh and sit eh down an ave oh eh little beerer to, the eh damn good Army, eh, Corp-al."

Peter I could see had a good load on, so I made some excuse and promised to see him later.

That night a hospital ship arrived from Basra full of wounded. Another attempt had been made to advance on Kut, but we were repulsed again. I went on board to have a look 'round. Most of the wounded were in a bad way. Several had died and were buried at sea; several operations had to be performed and the limbs thrown overboard. Some had lost a leg or an arm, others had a hand missing, and some were blind, having lost both eyes. Most of those poor fellows were cheerful, full of talk, and thankful to be alive. The next day they were drafted off to hospitals in Bombay.

My leave having expired, I was ordered to get aboard the B1 steamer *Ellenga* and in due time arrived back at Basra. My other three pals never turned up, and I saw no more of them, which didn't surprise me as Army life was too uncertain. Orders were made and canceled with a swipe of the pen, and a soldier never knew where he was likely to be from day to day. A soldier's goodbye and promises were just mere words only and meant nothing, especially in war time.

On reporting myself at GHQ, I was told to go to the headquarters of the general in charge of lines of communication where I was to take over a cruiser launch belonging to that office. I quite expected that I was going to be sent back to the front. But no, I was to be employed at Basra and came under the orders of the ADC of that particular branch, which was better than I'd hoped for, as I felt no longing for any more front-line work. Before taking over my duties, I had to present myself to the medical officer for the compulsory procedure of the Army short-arm inspection to see that I was free of all disease. All soldiers returning from leave were subject to that examination.

Back with the Fighting Forces

The launch had a crew of three including myself. I had a young soldier of the Warwickshire Regiment: one of the survivors of the Gallipoli mess up who had already made the acquaintance of the Turks. He came from the Midlands of England, and his language was so broad that I could barely understand what he was talking about. When I shouted to him to go ahead, he'd often put the engine in reverse, and many times we were on the verge of disaster. His nerves were all shot. At the sound of a petrol can dropping or the least bang of some article, he'd nearly jump out of the boat. That was why he'd been assigned to base duty. The other member of the crew was a native of the RIM. His duties were to jump ashore and hold the launch while loading or unloading passengers.

Troops were pouring into Basra every day and were rushed up to the front. Many shallow-draught boats armed with large guns and more airplanes had arrived. A large contingent of Australian nurses had also put in an appearance and had taken over the hospitals. Those pretty girls could be seen tripping about in their short-skirted uniforms on the dusty roads, escorted by smart-looking officers.

Our army at the front was at a standstill, neither side attempting to make any moves, due, no doubt, to the climatic conditions, what was known as the date-ripening season, which was accompanied with extreme heat waves. The troops were suffering terribly from thirst and other deprivations out on the open desert without so much as a fig leaf to shade them.

My duties consisted of taking certain staff officers out to the ships as they arrived. On Sundays I'd take the general up the river where he attended divine service in the open air in the shade of the trees. Sometimes in the dusk of the evening, I'd take a company of officers and nurses up one of the creeks near Basra. They'd get out and walk some distance away amongst the trees. I could plainly hear their laughing and giggles as they appeared to be enjoying themselves. Some of those young ladies were evidently out for a tea party while others were matrimonial bent; a few were trying to consciously perform their respective duties. After a few months, some of them could be seen with their bags and baggage, proceeding towards a homeward-bound steamer. Just a little heavier in mind and body.

One night my engineer failed to return to our little reed hut which we called our quarters, and of course as our services were required the next morning, I had to report his absence to the ADC, who smiled at me and said it was all right as he knew where my engineer was. Almost midday he showed up and appeared half scared out of his wits. He said he had just been released from the guard room at Ashar barrack where he had been locked up. This is his story, which no doubt was quite feasible:

"I was out in Basra, enjoying a few drinks, when I was approached by an Arab boy who wanted to know if I'd come and see his sister, so off I went and followed this kid who guided me to a house in one of the alleyways. Inside were two Armenian women, and having a few drinks under my belt, I proved an easy mark for them. I'd no sooner handed over some money when there was a big *bang*, and the door flew open. There stood two big military police who pulled me out and marched me to the guard room where I was charged with being found in company with a prostitute. Next morning they'd added the word 'drunk' against me. Then I was hauled in front of the commandant, a big beefy face looking old bastard, who said he was going to sentence me to No. 1 field punishment, but when I told him I was the general's motor launch driver, he climbed down a peg and telephoned through to ask the ADC if they required my services anymore. The ADC must be a good fellow, for he phoned back and said, 'Yes, send him back at once. He's just the man we want.'

So the beef gormandiser turns to me and says, 'Fortunate for you, young fellow, but we're determined to put a stop to this sort of thing. I shall fine you 30 days' pay under royal warrant. Now report back immediately to your duties.'"

That appeared to be one of the corrupt money-making schemes which was being worked between those women and the police, and the poor soldier had to pay in addition to being punished.

"How much did you give these women?" I asked him.

"That's the worst part of it. I paid five rupees and did no more than see their faces."

Just another day in the life of a soldier.

Sick men returning from the front brought little bits of news. They said it was getting unbearable up there, military discipline was being strictly enforced, court-martials were frequently held, and soldiers were being severely punished for the most minor offenses. In some cases, men had faced firing squads.

After a few months of work for the Basra ADC, I was ordered one morning to report myself to the adjutant general's office. I was told that I'd been transferred to the RE with the rank of sapper and was to report to that office at once for duty. I told him that I already belonged to the Norfolk Regiment.

"No you don't, no longer," the sergeant told me. "Your regiment exists in name only, and you're automatically transferred to the RE. Your depot is now at Chatham, England. Besides, you ought to consider yourself lucky. Your pay will be increased to more than double what you're receiving now." He believed a sapper's pay was about six shillings a day, about a dollar and a half American money.

So with all that sticking in my head, I made my way back to HQ and packed up my kit. I saw the ADC, and he told me he had applied to retain my services, but his request had been turned down. He allowed me the use of the launch to take me up to Makina, the other side of Basra, where my new HQ was located. I thanked him and was soon in the company of my new comrades. They told me I was just in time as they were leaving that night for the front with new searchlight outfits. There were about 18 of us including NCOs, all young fellows not more than 20 years of age. They had only just come out from England, and what I could gather, most of them were motion-picture operators. One of them was the very image of Charlie Chaplin, so he became known to us as Charlie. Our captain was an old Indian Army officer, having been promoted to his present rank from staff sergeant. He recognized me and said he had seen me several times at Nasiriyeh. It was he who had charge of blowing up the bund which had helped General Gorringe's advance. He told me to put the lance stripe up and would see that I got paid for it from the date of my transfer to the RE.

"You understand, Corporal, that these young fellows are quite green to Army life, and they need a few old soldiers like yourself to help them along a bit. So be careful how you treat them, and if at any time you need anything, let me know and I'll do all I can for you. I shall be coming with you tonight."

"Now," he said. "Take two men and hire a bellam, go to Strick Seolts, buy me one case of beer and one case of Scotch whiskey, and put them on board the T3 with the rest of our equipment. Don't expose it if you can help it."

"Wait a moment," he said as he went toward the staff sergeant. "Make it two cases of whiskey," he said and handed me 50 rupees in notes. "Get yourself a drink while you're out; I don't know when we shall get the next."

My initiation into the RE was celebrated that night while proceeding up the Shatt-al-Arab en route to the front. We were a happy group, having a small tug all to ourselves. I'd bought myself a case of beer and six bottles of whiskey which I distributed amongst the boys. Those youngsters were new to the war game and were anxious to see the front. They had never heard a shot fired, and after they had a few drinks, they started a little concert, each man being compelled to sing a song. After a while, the captain came out and cheerfully joined in the party.

We travelled day and night and stopped at Amara for a day while the tug took on coal. The captain gave us permission to go ashore for a couple of hours for a little exercise. Next day we arrived at Sheikh Sa'ad where we were to unload and erect one of our lights. There we built a large pyramid about 50 feet high, which took a few days and a lot of hard work as that pyramid had to be made with sacks filled with sand. On top was placed a large searchlight. After the light was in running order, I had orders to proceed up the river to Twin Canals, a small camp close to the rear of our lines on the right bank, and erect another light under the directions and instructions of the OC of that camp, whose orders I was to obey. The OC told me the camp was being troubled every night with a group of snipers, and several of his men had been wounded. So we got our light fixed, and strange to say, the snipers never appeared again.

In February 1917, the advance on Sonnaiyat was commenced, and after two days' fierce fighting, the Turks were driven from their impregnable fortifications and were fleeing in disorder towards Baghdad. Our troops and riverboats pursued them as far as Aziziye, a few miles southeast of Baghdad. Our Navy monitors got ahead of the Turks, and those who didn't surrender were shot down. We captured several Turkish boats and recovered several of our own which had been lost in General Townshend's battle at Kut.

A few days later, the Turks tried desperately to check our advance, but they were now about demoralized, and our army entered Baghdad on 12 March 1917. The Turks were then fleeing toward Mosul, closely followed by our troops. At Twin Canals, a large Turkish prisoner camp was built to accommodate the many thousands we had captured. They were put to work to clean up the battlefields and bury the dead. Kut was a heap of ashes, having been burnt to the ground by the Turks. For days afterwards, boatloads of our wounded were being conveyed to the hospitals at Amara and Basra.

We were next ordered to rush our two searchlights to Fao right away, back to the mouth of the Shatt-al-Arab and Persian Gulf. It was feared that German submarines would be operating in that quarter as there was quite a lot of shipping between eastern ports and Basra; large ships with stores of war materials were arriving from Japan, Australia, and India. Some of the ships had to be unloaded at the bar on account of their high draughts. So away we rushed, only calling in at Basra for provisions.

Fao was occupied by a small detachment of native infantry with half a dozen 18-pounders mounted near the banks of the river. There were a few old brick buildings, and those we made our quarters, got to work, and soon had our lights in working order. Those lights were kept running all night, playing the beam up and down the river, but never a submarine showed up. After a while, our lights were replaced by larger and more powerful plants. When those arrived, we were kept busy getting them laid down. The engines and dynamos were to have cement beds which ordinarily could be made in the earth, but as it was all sand and we could only dig about a foot before we came to water, the cement foundations had to be built on the sand upwards. That work proved quite an experiment as it was expected that on starting up, the engine would pull the dynamo off its seat, but no, the demi was with us, and it worked fine. From those generating plants we wired the buildings and little hospital, and so we had our own electric light.

Then somebody sent us an old ice machine, but we didn't have much luck with it. None of us knew much about that class of machine, but we did our best by trying to follow the instructions in the books. We were all anxious to get the machine going as ice would be a godsend and was a great necessity. What little ice we did get we had to beg from the ships which passed. Our ice machine was a failure. The only thing we managed to turn out was hot water. So one day an ice machine mechanic came down from Basra and got our machine going. He wanted to know what sort of engineers we called ourselves because we couldn't fix a poor little ice machine. We politely told him to knuckle under, or we would push him in the river.

In that isolated little spot, we had to make our own amusements as it looked very much as if we were to stay there for the duration of the war. We were as comfortable as it was possibly to be under the circumstances. We had made ourselves some bed cots out of lengths of two-by-four wood and stretched over with sacks. Our greatest pests were sand flies. It seemed as if they came across the desert and finding their passage blocked by the sea, settled down in our little spot to torment everybody. We couldn't catch them because they were invisible, and yet there were millions of them. They started attacking at nighttime and were more irritating than bugs or flies. Our water was brackish and not fit to drink; the water in the Shatt-al-Arab was seawater and no good to us. Our little garrison numbered about 50 all told, including officers and a doctor. The doctor was a native of India, what they called an apothecary. He smoked and drank and often told us native fairy tales to help while away the time. The Arabs would come to him for treatment when they were sick. One day a little Arab girl was brought to him for treatment, suffering from burnt eyes. Some of her people had burnt the poor girl's eyes out with hot wires for some breach in Arab rules. Of course the doctor could do nothing but only try to relieve her pain. She must have been a girl about 14 years old. Her punishment, I was told, was only one of the Arab methods.

Our rations came down from Basra by boat once a week, and our captain would sometimes include a case of beer. We used to look forward to those days as if we were going to a party because we were sure of some nice new bread and other kinds of eatables. There was nothing to purchase in Fao, and money was useless, so we had to depend on what was sent from Basra. Most of the Arab population had disappeared and taken their belongings with them soon after we arrived and took over their houses, which numbered about a dozen, so we were entirely on our own. Our nearest neighbors were at Koweit, an Arab town a few miles away and situated on the Gulf.

Our staff sergeant was taken suddenly ill and died. The doctor said it was heart failure. We tried to find a burial ground for him, but everywhere we dug was water, so we sewed him up in some blankets weighted with some angle irons, took him out to sea, and quietly dropped him over the side of the tug into the Persian Gulf. From that time, our little company began to diminish; most every day there was a new case of sickness. Hospital ships were stopped and the sick taken on board suffering from high fever. The doctor said it was due to the drinking water and sand flies.

My turn came at last. One morning found me in our little hospital, suffering from the same disease, and a day or two later I was placed on board a hospital ship where I remained to be invalided back to India. The day the ship left, as I lay in my little cot, I watched the date palms flow past my porthole in the side of the ship, and somehow I knew I was bidding goodbye to Mesopotamia for the last time. I didn't feel sorry, only weak and tired. During the ten-day voyage, I slept most of the time, glad to be freed from the irritating vermin I'd left behind. The ship seemed loaded. All the cots were occupied; most of the soldiers were bed patients.

On arrival at Bombay, we were all tagged with our name, regiment, and disease we were suffering from. The task of unloading was in the hands of the shore authorities. Myself and others who could walk ashore left first. On our entering the shed, our tags were examined, and we were drafted off in cars to various hospitals in the city. I was amongst a party which was sent to the Parsee hospital on Malabar Hill where we could look out of the windows and see the Parsee Tower of Silence and the birds of prey perched on top, waiting patiently for their next meal to come along. I wondered if the Tower would be our last resting place. Under the treatment received at hospital, I made a swift recovery, and after a couple of weeks I was feeling fit to leave the hospital although by my looks I appeared to be still a very sick man. My features were pale and of a yellowish colour, and I looked more like a Chinaman than an English one. We had plenty of good food, and the ladies would bring their cars in the evenings and take us out for little trips into the country around the city, which was greatly appreciated by all of us war-worn Tommies. Some ladies who didn't own cars would hire a taxi and take us out. In that way we made many pleasant friendships which still remain beautiful memories of Bombay. As we became convalescent, we had to leave the hospital to make room for new arrivals which were continually pouring in.

So in due course, I found myself amongst a group which was drafted to Secunderabad, supposed to be a semiconvalescent station in central India. Upon our arrival there, we were quartered in an old fort infested with snakes, mongooses, and mosquitoes. After a few weeks, I was stricken with malaria and carried off to hospital again where I was to remain in a critical condition for six months. My blood tests proved that I was practically eaten up with malaria. Twice I was taken out on the verandah, placed in the corner with a red screen 'round the bed, and given up for lost. But I felt that I didn't want to die. One day I was placed on a stretcher, taken to another building, and placed upon a cloth-covered bench. I must admit I felt a little scared and wondered what was going to happen to me. I had a thought that they were going to kill me off. As I lay there on my back, my eyes wandered 'round the room. I could see large bottles full of some kind of medicine with long tubes attached to them. A doctor and a nurse came in. The nurse got busy at once and with some instrument she opened one of my veins near the muscle of my right arm. The doctor then placed a small silver tube in the hole and attached the end of one of the tubes. He then turned a little tap, and I could see the contents of the bottle lowering as it emptied itself into my body. During that time I had the sensation of a very pleasing taste in my mouth. The puncture in my arm was then bound up, the doctor asked me if I was feeling all right, and he assured me that I'd soon be well again.

I must admit that from that moment I began to feel a new man, every day improving in appearance. I was put on special diets. Several times during the days that followed, doctors would come and see me and ask how I was feeling. They would then stand away out of my hearing and laugh and talk together, occasionally pointing in my direction. Sometime after I found out that it was a kill-or-cure treatment they had given me, and so I had refused to give up the ghost. I made a speedy recovery; my blood tests proved negative. My nurse, a colonel's wife in the RE, was so pleased at my recovery that I thought she was going to kiss me once or twice. When I was fit to get about, she took me to her home for tea and got me to tell her all about Mesopotamia. She said her husband was still out there on the general staff and was now in Baghdad.

One day the parson came to see me. I saw him coming and laughed, telling him that he was too late but that I nearly needed his services a few days back. He held my hand and said, "So you're the young man who refused to die." He told me that I was the most extraordinary case in the hospital and that nobody had been known to live with such temperatures as I'd had. But he said, "You know that old soldiers never die." As he was going away, he dropped a bar of chocolate and a package of cigarettes on my bed. "Hurry up and get out of hospital," he said. "They're going to send you to the hills."

So one morning in company with a few more men, I was placed on the train for Willington, a convalescent station and the highest point in southern India. Most of the European women went there during the hot season and left their husbands behind to get on with their jobs. On the railway journey we had to pass through some part of the Nizam's dominions and saw the natives at work collecting the toddy from the tall trees of which there must have been millions. Each tree represented one rupee per year in taxes which went to His Exalted Highness. Bananas were also growing in abundance and could be purchased from the native peddlers in huge bunches for a few annas.

The trains in India never seemed to be in a hurry. Upon arriving at a station, nobody knew when the train was likely to start again; it was quite possible to be that day or perhaps the next, and nobody seemed to care. The stations were usually packed with natives who had come to see the train come in. Women and little kiddies with big bellies, who looked as if they had just eaten a big feed of raw rice and water, causing them to swell up to an enormous size, looked like comical creatures as they ran around, staring out of big black eyes, asking for baksheesh, the only word which seemed to be popular amongst the natives. They seemed to think a white person was made of baksheesh.

At last we arrived at the junction where we changed for the railway with its quaint little carriages which was to take us up the hills. Those trains crept along in a circular route as they wound around the mountains and finally reached the terminus at Ootyrumund, some thousands of feet above the plains. About half-way up, we could feel the change in the atmosphere and were compelled to button up to keep warm. During that journey, nothing was seen, only the steep sides of ravines running with water, until we reached Willington, a small plateau surrounded by mountain peaks. We tumbled out of the carriages and ran around in the perfect sunshine to get warmed up. We were then taken in cars to Badger Hill Camp, a combination of wooden huts which had been built to accommodate war convalescents. Beautiful wildflowers and ferns were in abundance everywhere, the like of which I'd only seen in England. The scent of the tall eucalyptus trees filled the air, bushes were full of blackberries, and birds of a lovely plumage could be seen, including parrots and sparrows. I never could imagine that such a wonderful place existed in India, and of course I was already beginning to wonder how long I was going to be permitted to stay there. Next day we all had to visit the medical officer, who was a big, burly-featured Australian but quite different from the "don't yer know" type of British officer. His name was Major Portor. First thing he said was, "Sit down and tell me how you feel." I told him I was feeling fine. He then asked me if I'd like to go into the hospital.

"No, Sir," I said. "I've only just come out and want to get a little fresh air."

"Ah," he said. "That's what they all say, but you look far from being well. I don't like the colour of your face. Do you drink beer?" he asked me.

"Oh, yes," I replied. "Sometimes."

"Well, drink as much beer as you like, but cut out smoking cigarettes. If you smoke at all, try a pipe."

He then told me to report to him every morning to have my temperature taken and to be careful not to catch cold.

The next two months passed like a dream, the happiest I ever spent as a soldier in the British Army. We indulged in hockey and football matches, went for long rambles up hills and down dales. There were no restrictions. We were allowed to go wherever we pleased. There were no roll calls except once a week, when we were required to attend the pay office to receive our pay. Quite a different Army to what I'd been used to, but like other good things, it had to come to an end to make room for others. And all too soon I found myself listed to rejoin my unit which was then temporarily quartered at Bangalore in a canvas camp. The day I left Willington, my chums made me a gift of a little fox terrier puppy which was my constant companion for the remainder of my stay in India. That little fellow could do all kinds of tricks, including beg, borrow, and steal, and became a great favourite with my future comrades.

My dog and I eventually arrived at the great Bangalore where I found my corps was stationed about three miles out on the other side of the city, living in great Eastern-pattern tents. The climate was very warm and felt like coming from the North Pole to the equator to me. On the top of a huge flag staff was a sign which read "Gaza Camp, RE Training Depot." I knew then that I'd struck the right trail and reached my new home. The camp was made up of two classes, No. 1 and No. 2. No. 2 was composed of convalescents like myself, and No. 1 was A-1 men who did all the duties. It took me a few days to get climatized, and after a few weeks I was transferred to No. 1 for ordinary duties. There were no drills or parades except the Sunday morning parade when we were marched to church some three miles away to be accused by the parson of reading the hymn books upside down. Most of the men would be indulging in crap games during the sermon period. During the week we were mostly employed repairing the rifle range for about four hours each day, but that work was only a farce, just a matter of something to put in the weekly report to be submitted to HQ. Most of the men were spending those four hours scouting 'round the country, looking for sand rats in female form. Every morning at eight o'clock we would march off to the range about two miles distance, accompanied by a group of dogs, my terrier amongst them.

The evenings would find us either in the canteen or out in the city where a couple of houses of ill fame were doing a thriving business amongst the troops. It was then that the worldwide influenza epidemic hit Bangalore. Every day, men were being taken to hospital, only to live for a few hours. We were turning out two and three times a day to attend military funerals until we were all scared, wondering who would be next. The attacks were so sudden that a soldier would feel all right today, and the next, he'd be dead, death and burial taking place the same day. Nobody was kept for two sunsets in India.

One day myself and a couple of pals visited the civil jail where for a couple of rupees, a guard would show us 'round that institution. In one section we saw the prisoners making beautiful carpets. They made motions to us, indicating they wanted a cigarette, so I asked the guard if I could give them some.

"Oh yes, sahib," and I was about to hand a package to one of them when the guard grabbed them from my hand. "Nay, sahib," he said. "Only give one cigarette to each man, or they will all fight and maybe kill me."

So I had to hand those cigarettes out one at a time to the prisoners, who were soon blowing large clouds of smoke through their hands in native fashion. I asked the guard if tobacco was issued to the prisoners.

"Nay, sahib, only what visitors give them."

I asked him if they had many visitors. He said, "Nay, sahib, only soldier man come here and visit. The prisoners all like soldier man to come."

We then saw the carpenters at work, making Army tables and chairs; at another place they were making sacks. Then the guard took us to some very small cells, just room enough for a man to lay down and stand up and about the width of an ordinary door. Through a little grate could be seen a naked man, sitting on the stone floor beside a large stone at which he was chipping away small pieces with a chisel and hammer. The sweat was running down his body through little channels of brick dust.

"Him very bad man sahib," said the guard to me, "Him lunatic crazy man, kill other man."

"But why do you let him have a chisel and hammer?" I asked him. "He may kill himself."

"That's all right, sahib; we no have to keep him, then." He said the man had been in that cell for 15 years.

"Do you hang people here?" I asked him.

"Oh, yes, sahib, you come, me show you."

We followed him down a slight incline to where there were three isolated cells, and in each one was a murderer. At the end was the scaffold built over a cement hole where the body dropped through. The rope was still dangling there, and I noticed the noose was plastered in what appeared to be dry blood. So I asked the guard if they didn't use a new rope each time.

"Nay, sahib, same rope all time unless rope break." Then he pointed to two of the cells. "Them two men are brothers; we hang them tonight. They kill father and mother and take all rupees, but we ketch 'em, sahib. Very bad men."

Just as we were leaving the prison, we encountered a batch of about 20 prisoners all shackled together with chains, guarded by an armed party with fixed bayonets. Most of the natives of India went to prison for their crimes, it being impossible for them to pay fines.

The weeks dwindled by and began to get monotonous for the want of a change. One day there was a rumour that we were going to be rushed up to the northwest frontier on account of some trouble up there, but that move didn't materialize and at last, about ten o'clock that night, we got the news that the armistice was signed. That was enough; the whole camp went mad with joy. Soldiers demanded that the canteen be thrown open. When that demand was refused, they raided the place, burst open the doors, and rolled all the barrels out to the parade ground. There the tops were knocked in and a free-for-all was started. Bottles of whiskey mysteriously appeared from somewhere, and the celebrations continued well into the next day, but that was only a small preliminary start. The city's inhabitants took up the call, and for one whole week there was great rejoicing every day on the miadan in the centre of the city. Military bands turned out and played dance tunes for the great multitude of dancers. High and low, rich and poor, mingled together discussing the glad tidings. Such a scene. It was hardly believable that the natives were so patriotic. Native soldiers paraded the streets with monkeys and parrots on their shoulders. The whole show came to an end with a big final gala day and a magnificent display of fireworks in which the Kaiser was burnt and so ended the armistice celebrations in Bangalore.

After the armistice explosion had died down, the troops became unsettled and were all clamouring to be sent home, but that was impossible on account of the low percentage of shipping which was then available and a great problem for the authorities. The men were on the verge of mutiny at times and would only obey orders after some hesitancy. That was a foolish attitude to take because it didn't help any; on the contrary, it may have retarded the movement because we were taken from the tents, placed in one of the vacant barracks, and made to do guards and picquets. One day a large contingent of troops arrived from Mesopotamia. Those troops had originally been booked to proceed to England, but for some reason they'd been dumped in India. They rebelled and refused to do anything in the nature of military duties. They threw all the barrack utensils out on the square including tables, chairs, bed cots, wash basins, etc. They were finally calmed down after being severely lectured by a general who promised that he'd not hesitate to use extreme measures if such nonsense didn't cease at once. From then on at periodical intervals and as shipping became available, small drafts of about 100 men would be dispatched to Bombay. At that time, there was a large demand for shipping all over the world, and everybody knew that ships were at a premium, the German submarines being largely at fault for that state of affairs. Large bounties were offered to professional soldiers to extend their service and immediately be promoted to NCO rank. A few men availed themselves of the opportunity, but professional soldiers were very few and far between. Most of the veterans were either dead or invalids like myself and no further use as a soldier. I'd volunteered to go up to the northwest frontier, also back to Mesopotamia, but my services were rejected on account of ill health although I was feeling as fit as a fiddle.

Homeward Bound

The day arrived when my name appeared in the list of a party which was to proceed to Bombay en route for dear old England. We were all given 100 rupees each and documents bearing the name of the demobilizing centre in England, usually located in a district nearest to the man's home. We had spent a couple of hours in the canteen, having parting drinks with our pals, and when the "fall in" sounded, most of us were more or less slightly illuminated but all in a cheerful mood. As we marched away from Cornwallis barracks, the only sound I heard was that of my little fox terrier who had set off a series of mournful yells. I'd given him away to the sergeant major with whom he was a great favourite. We had to march three miles to the station, carrying our kit bags and rifles slung over our shoulders. On the way, two or three dropped out, unable to keep up the pace. One old soldier with a couple of beery legs who was some way behind had fallen down and was struggling with his kit bag and rifle to balance himself. So I dropped back to help him along. He was in such a bad way that I commandeered a country cart to drive us to the station, but it took me nearly half an hour wrangling with the driver with the promise of plenty of baksheesh before I could get him to move. It was dark, and our party was well out of sight, and as I was on strange ground, I had to trust the driver of the bullocks cart who kept twisting the bullocks' tails and urging them on at greater speed. At last, we arrived at the station, but to my dismay I could see nothing of our party, and upon making inquiries, I was told my party was leaving by special train from a station about three miles away and had just departed. At that very moment a trainful of troops passed through. The station official said that was the train I was looking for and told me if I'd been a few minutes earlier, he could have pulled the train up for us.

What to do now? I didn't know. My pal, who was now sobered up, said, "Come on, let's go and have a drink."

So into the refreshment room we went and came in contact with a Parsee babu who told us that a passenger train would be leaving in an hour for Bombay. So we decided to board that train and take a chance. It was no use going back to camp and risk being court-martialed, so we passed the time sipping whiskey and soda and ordered a case of beer and sandwiches to be placed on the train. We secured a first-class European carriage to ourselves and once on the train very soon fell off to sleep. We were really better off than being cooped up in an uncomfortable troop train. During the journey we awoke at intervals to drink beer and eat sandwiches. A few miles from Bombay the collector awoke us and demanded our tickets. I told him an officer on the train had our tickets. The collector looked dubious but moved on and never bothered us again, and so we arrived at the Victoria Terminus Bombay where we at once hired a gharry to convey us to the docks. We were informed that a troop train wasn't due for another eight hours. We spent most of that time talking over our experiences with some of the embarkation staff in the canteen. There I was told that my old pal Peter had taken his discharge and had gone to Madras to take a job as inspector of native police. He had said that he preferred to stay in India alive than chance getting drowned by striking one of the mines that were infesting the shipping routes at sea. I never saw Peter or heard from him again. When the troop train arrived, we waited our chance, slipped in unseen, and mingled with the troops. At "roll call" every man was reported present. We had enjoyed a first-class trip, thanks to my pal's rickety legs.

As we shook the dust of India from our feet and slowly filed up the gangplank of the SS *Eksma,* we were each presented with two little packages from the ladies' organizations of India. My parcels contained a little bronze matchbox holder with a map of India and two sleeping suits, a product manufactured from India's cotton and made by native labour. Those two presents could only bring happy memories of that great country for years to come. Every night, on donning that suit, my mind would wander back to that land of mystery where I'd spent so many pleasant hours, hours which could never be forgotten.

It was raining very hard, and as we were pulled out of the docks, hardly a soul was to be seen, and we were soon lost to view in the mist created by the rain. The ship was overcrowded and accommodations bad; the only food available was potatoes, canned meat, and biscuits issued three times a day, washed down with water which had a salty flavour. Those inconveniences didn't bother us. We were going home; nothing else mattered. We would soon be free of Army rations.

As we moved into the Arabian Sea, we got the full force of the south-west monsoon which was blowing a hurricane with terrific force, and for six days the ship rolled and tossed about in mighty seas which threatened at any moment to swamp the ship and drown us all. The ship very often appeared to be standing on its nose, the propellers roaring around as they stood out of the water. All the troops were laying about on the decks on which they rolled for a week like a lot of dead sheep, suffering from seasickness and caring little about what happened to them. From stem to stern, the ship was a mass of slime except in places where the high seas had washed the decks. The days were as dark as the nights until I wondered if we were going to live to get through it. Nothing could be heard, only the howling winds and occasional roar of the propellers. The ship was dead as far as life was concerned, yet we had about 2,000 souls on board. The ship's boats would be quite inadequate and useless in such seas, but the good ship slowly plowed her way to calmer waters, and one morning we found ourselves steaming up the calm waters of the Red Sea towards the Gulf of Suez. At Suez the ship was unable to proceed any farther on account of bad leaks, and nobody knew until then how near we'd been to foundering. The ship's crew and all other available hands had been working hard night and day at the pumps. The captain feared the ship might break her back. At port we disembarked and remained two days while arrangements were being made to convey us to Port Said by rail. Nothing very important to report about Suez. We spent most of the time scrounging 'round, looking for something decent to eat and drink, but Suez seemed in a poor way. Apparently it had already been drained.

On arriving at Port Said, in the remains of what had been one huge camp, we were dumped to remain indefinitely to await ships to carry us on the next stage of our journey home. In that camp we became acquainted with Australian and Canadian soldiers, all waiting for ships to carry them home. That city was very uninviting and was as dry as the surrounding sands of the desert. The place had been skinned clean of everything by the never-ending departure of troops. The only food which could be purchased in the town was the daily supply of fresh fish which was caught in the Mediterranean Sea. There was of course the usual amusements and playthings to be found wherever soldiers were quartered, but Port Said would soon become a camp in name only. Where there had been thousands, only a few hundred remained, and those were employed cleaning up the remains of the once great camping ground, so well-known to the Australian soldiers during the war.

One morning we were hurried aboard the Dutch ship *Princess Juliana*, conveyed across the Mediterranean to Marseilles, and dumped in a camp high up in the hills. After a week there, we were packed into freight cars, conveyed across war-torn France to Bologne, and finally shipped across the English Channel to Dover where we were met at the landing stage by some ladies who presented us with chocolate and cigarettes. It was there that we said our good-byes and separated to go our different ways to our demobilization centres. Some few hours afterwards, I reported myself at Fleetwood in Essex, and there I was relieved of my rifle and equipment and given a bankbook with a deposit enclosed of 28 pounds. I was then given two pounds in cash and a railway ticket to my home, and shook hands with the officer who wished me luck in my return to civilian life.

I thanked him and saluted the uniform for the last time. A few moments afterwards, the gates of military discipline clanged behind me. Good-bye to the Army. The 28 pounds was just about enough to get myself rigged up in a decent civilian attire, and I found myself once again alone in London as I'd been some 15 years before, stoney broke and out of a job.

Appendix A

Frederick French's Certificate of Naturalization

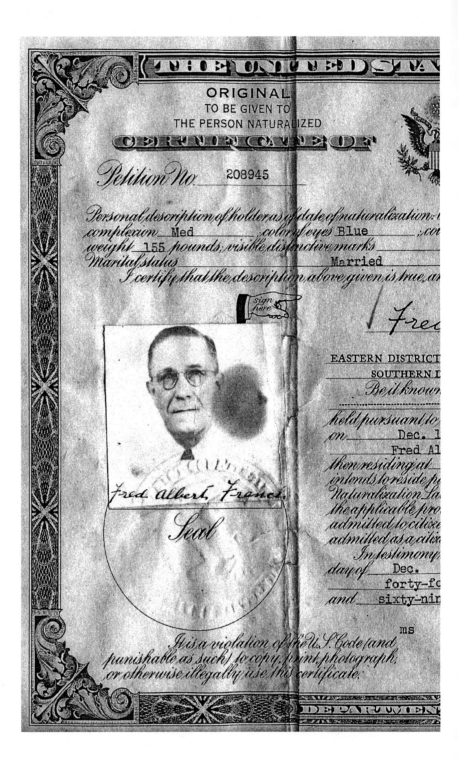

THE UNITED STA

ORIGINAL
TO BE GIVEN TO
THE PERSON NATURALIZED

CERTIFICATE OF

Petition No. 208945

Personal description of holder as of date of naturalization:
complexion Med *;color of eyes* Blue *;co*
weight 155 *pounds; visible distinctive marks*
Marital status Married
I certify that the description above given is true, an

✓ Fre

EASTERN DISTRICT
SOUTHERN D
Be it known

held pursuant to
on Dec. 1
Fred Al
then residing at
intends to reside p
Naturalization La
the applicable pro
admitted to citize
admitted as a citiz
In testimony
day of Dec.
forty-fo
and sixty-nin

ms

Fred Albert Francis

Seal

*It is a violation of the U.S. Code (and
punishable as such) to copy, print, photograph,
or otherwise illegally use this certificate.*

DEPARTMEN

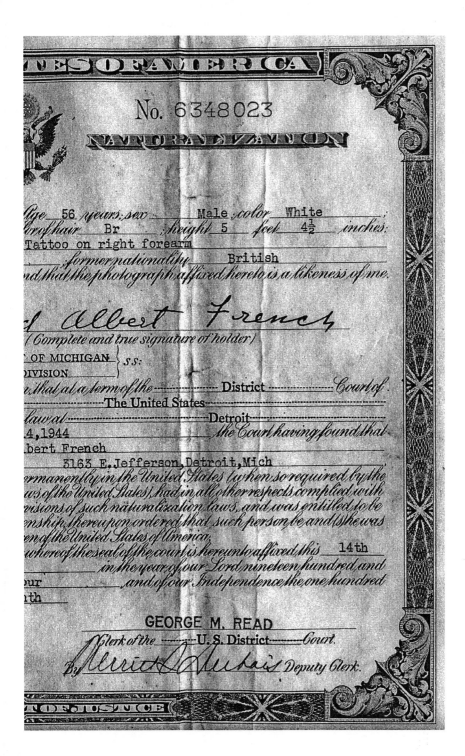

TES OF AMERICA

No. 6348023

NATURALIZATION

Age 56 years; sex Male ; color White ;
or of hair Br ; height 5 feet 4½ inches;
Tattoo on right forearm
former nationality British
and that the photograph affixed hereto is a likeness of me.

Albert French

(Complete and true signature of holder)

OF MICHIGAN ⎱ ss:
DIVISION ⎰

that at a term of the District Court of
The United States
law at Detroit
4, 1944 the Court having found that
bert French
5163 E. Jefferson, Detroit, Mich
ermanently in the United States (when so required by the
ws of the United States), had in all other respects complied with
visions of such naturalization laws, and was entitled to be
nship, thereupon ordered that such person be and (s)he was
en of the United States of America.
whereof the seal of the court is hereunto affixed this 14th
in the year of our Lord nineteen hundred and
ur and of our Independence the one hundred
th

GEORGE M. READ

Clerk of the U. S. District Court.
By Deputy Clerk.

OF JUSTICE

Appendix B

Original Manuscript Pages

"Soldier of the King," the first chapter of *Tommy Adkins*, is includededed here to allow readers to see French's original manuscript. Although the pages are legible, words on the reverse side bleed through a bit and the pencil point in which the original was composed gets thick in places; some parts are therefore difficult to read. Even so, reviewing these pages is well worth a reader's effort.

Soldier of the King

Stoney broke and alone in London
thats how I found myself one day some years
before the great war, what a predicament to
to be in, not knowing were my next meal was
coming from. I was one of those young fellows
who never did trouble to look ahead, why
should I bother, I was possessed with all the
best gifts that god could bestow on any
person, strength and health

I had lost my job, and work at
that time was very hard to find especially in
the country where I came from, so with a few
pounds I came to London with the good intention
of finding myself work, I had never been in
London before and was green to city life
I suppose I was a country pumpkin coming to
town, Well London looked mighty good to
me for a day or two, I thought surely this was
the place to land a job with lots of people
all hustling to and fro, traffic everywhere,
everybody seemed to be busy, nicely dressed
men and women, their nice clothes seemed to be
so different to my country made suit. I
did the rounds applying here and there where

B-2

I thought I stood a possible chance, but no not today, the same results from the employment offices, with which London is flooded, I wondered how they maintained their places if they never had any jobs to offer but all I got was "come in again to morrow", after days of this my patience finally got eschausted. I didnt know wether to return home anyhow I decided to enjoy myself before deciding what to do, perhaps fate would do something, so I let myself go as far as my remaining finances would permit, I went to shows, music halls, most of the theatres in — cluding a chance meeting with some of the pretty London girls untill my eschequeers refused any futher embursements, and so there I was face to face with nothing, I could not go home because I had no fare and I couldnt think of Shankes pony,

As I was walking slowly along the sidewalk in the vicinity of Trafalger Sq. wondering what I should do, my eyes caught sight of a big poster outside of a large building which read in large type" Join the army and become a man" then followed good pay free rations hospitals and medical attention, then under this there was all kinds of soldiers some on horses

and some on foot all dressed up in their
smart looking uniforms, there was big
dragoons, Lancers, Engineers, Artillery with
big guns Medical corps Infantrymen with
rifles and all the rest of the British Army
including generals and majors all decked up
in their pretty clothes

As I stood there gazing at this
a soldier came to the doorway and beconed to
me, hello young fellow want to join the army
come right in here and let me look you over
and before I had time to look around he
had pushed me into his office, sit down
he said, then he goes on, ever been in the
army before, no sir I said, well it dont matter
much if you was only you dont have to tell me
understand, yes sir I understand, and you dont
have to call me sir you can save that for
the officers, I'm only a recruiting Sergeant
and my job is to get smart young fellows
like you to join his Majestys Army, but
I said I dont know anything about the
Army I never worked for the army before
Dont worry about that young man, you
dont have to know anything in the army
all you have to do is to Obey orders and

do as you are told in fact we ~~learn~~ teach you
every thing, and give your nothing, I mean
we give you everything you want, We
pay you, feed you give you a gun to play
with, when you are sick, we have nice hospitals
and doctors, and pretty nurses to tuck you
in at night, now ~~what~~ more do ~~you want~~
a gentlemans life, ~~thats what~~ it is and what
more if you happen to be alive at the end
of twenty years the king gives you a couple
a pound a week to get out of the Army and
stay out, there doesnt ~~that sound~~ pretty good
retired pensioner thats what they call it.
He kept rattling on all about the army that
I didnt understand, ...

Now young man come into this
room and let me run the tape round you
Here I stripped and was measured weighted
and had to hop on one leg then the other and
went through a few more motions and was
pronounced fit. He got me to sign a
few Army documents and told me to be
there at ten oclock the following morning
to see the doctor who would test my heart
and then it wouldnt be long before I was
a full blown soldier. With that he

gave me a shilling (25¢) and took me to the canteen and filled me up with bread and cheese and beer, told me where to sleep that night and left me

That night I spent my shilling in the canteen drinking beer which I shared with a few soldiers who dropped in and seemed quite pleased to help me with my beer. One soldier had two medals and I asked him what they were for. Ah young man I am very proud of these medals you can only get these on very special occasions This one was awarded to me for making Army puddings. All soldiers like lots of pudding so one year the king had more soldiers than he needed so he told me to give them plenty of pudding with the result that they all got sick and died, you see they were suffering from puddingitis. This other medal is called the Bethlehem star it was given to me by the shah of Persia. One day when he was over here trying to count all the guns we have he had a little sack full of these stars there supposed to be lucky and possess the magic charm of turning water into wine but it didn't work in this country. Next morning the canteen man called me about seven and gave me a job

B-6

to wash a few dishes and sweep the floor, for this he gave me my breakfast. At ten oclock the recruiting Sergt came for me to get prepared for the doctor who arrived about twelve. I went through the same motions as the day before was sworn in by taking the oaths and had become a faithful soldier of the king whom I was to serve, for twelve years. The sergt gave me half a crown and told me the remainder of the day was a holiday, I was to report to him the following day at ten when I would be dispatched to the depot of my regiment Youre in the army now he said and are subject to military law, what that was I did not know, I went back to the canteen and helped to serve the food and beer, so far as I could see the army appeared to be alright up to now

Next day the Sergt took me to the railway station got my ticket gave me another half a crown 50¢ and some papers in an official envelope and told me to report myself to the Sergt in charge of the guard room at Warley barracks, he laughed and said he hoped to see me a full blown General some day, but he said if you dont like the army come and see him and he would fix me up in some other regiment I thought this was pretty good of him with that he said so-long and good luck,

Soon I arrived at Warley barracks which is only a few miles from the east side of London. It was getting dark so I was told to find the store keeper and get my bedding, after numerious inquiries and searching several barrack rooms I located the storekeeper half drunk in the canteen Hello youngster, he greeted me got any money if not you aint getting no bedding tonight. but I protested the sergt said you would give me my bedding, to hell with the sergt im sergt of the bedding, come and sit down kid and stick a couple o pints o beers and youll find that I can do yer quite a lot of little favours This storekeeper surely had a thirst for beer pint after pint he would consume and I could not move him until closeing time. come along with me youngster I'll put you in the storeroom for tonight and fix you up in the morning, he opened a door and pushed me in saying he would see me in the morning with that he closed and locked the door on the outside. It was dark in this room but luckily I had a box of matches and could see stacks of little square mattresses and lots of blankets so being tired I curled up amongst these and fell into a sound sleep. Some

hours later, I was awakened by the sound of a
bugle, soon afterwards the storekeeper appeared
hello kid had a good sleep, he gave me my
bedding and told me to take it to the recruits
room just across the way, I should find a
corporal there who would take care of me. The
room was a large one with about thirty beds each side
with long tables down the centre and forms to
sit on. This room was full of recruits they were
all busy making up beds and sweeping the room
although it was very cold all the windows were
open but the soldiers seemed happy, some were
whistling others were trying their voices at singing
the latest songs, at my appearance they stood
and stared for a moment and then greeted me
with one long yell, and come in chum and
make yourself at home if you have come to
stop, then a trumpet sounded there was another
yell, some half dozen of these men disappeared
with buckets and trays to return in a few minutes
with steaming hot tea and bread, come on
rookie and muck in they called to me, there was
bread and large cans of jam washed down with what
was supposed to be tea, but tasted as if somebody
had been washing there socks in it, this I found
out consisted of breakfast, after this meal

was over, a corporal appeared and called out my name, he showed me a little slip of paper with my number rank and name printed upon it, he took me to the Medical Inspection room, were I was again subject to an examination, this I found out was just a matter of routine, for new recruits it seemed to me just to get acquainted with Medical Officers.

The best part of this day was taken up in getting rigged up with my uniform and necessaries. From the clothing stores to the tailors shop to get fitted and alterations made. I was then issued with all the different articles that go to make a British soldiers outfit, I never had so many things before in all my life, the outfit composed of the following, four suits, two Khaki suits one canvas suit and one dress suit made of red material with white collar and cuffs with blue trousers and red stripe three woollen shirts three pairs woollen socks two pairs of heavy boots one pair canvas slippers boot brushes, hair brush, comb shaving brush and razor cleaning brush and polish for brass work, one large overcoat and lots of other gear for cleaning purposes and I began to wonder how I was going to take care of all this stuff, I didn't have to wonder very long because I soon found out that

somebody else was takeing care of it for me,
that same day two pairs of my socks mysteriously
disappeared. My unform had to be neatly foled
up in a certain way and placed on a shelf over
my bed cot, the other things were kept in a box
which was placed at the foot of the bed, I was
advised to buy a lock and keep the box locked up
at all times, I was now in uniform and al -
-though I was supposed to have been fitted
I did not feel so very comfortable, when I looked
down I could see that my trousers looked more
like a concertina, but I was told that for
a small fee the tailor would put that all right
my shoes too, seemed a few sizes to large which
the shoemaker would change for a slightly used
pair that would be more comfortable and I found
that I could get almost any thing done for a small fee
but as I had no fee at that time I had to be content
to walk around looking something like a scarecrow
I found that by wearing my three shirts, it helped
to fill out my Khaki jacket so it didnt look
to bad, but I made up my mind that I would
have to gove the tailor his little fee as soon as I
could for some reason or other my size had been
sort of over estimated and it was up to me to
pay for alterations, oh well I suppose thats a

B-11

way they have in the Army.

The following day for the benefit of the last joined recruits a sergt gave us a lecture on the days routine as laid down in rules and regulations, he had us all seated round the tables himself standing at the end and every now and then striking the table with his cane as though putting emphasis upon his words, he started off–

Now my lads I want you to pay particular attention to what I am going to tell you and to remember it because this lecture is only given once. This life that you are about to enter is all new to you and is quite altogether different from what you have been used to, most of you have only just left your mothers apron strings, and the profession you have now entered upon is not an easy one as you will no doubt find out, it calls for pluck, strength, endureance, patience, and obedience, you have become part of that great fighting machine that holds the great British Empire together and there will be times when you will be called upon to use tact and initiative in cases of great importance and responsibility and dont forget that obedience is one of the most important rules laid down, obey all orders given by a superior officer, your complaints if any will always be heard after and justly delt with. Now get that well fixed into your heads, At this point an Officer enters the room, The Sergt shouts attention, salutes the officer and reports all present, the officer salutes back and says 'carry on sergt'

This is what is known as an infantry depot, here you will be gradually trained into the making of a good all round soldier of the king. When you leave this depot it will be to join your regiment in what ever particlar part of the world it may be quartered, there you will find friendship and comradeship seldom found elsewhere and wherever you see the union jack flying you are just as good as being in your own home, but yours happiness parcially depends upon youself and by useing a little sound judgment no effects have been spared to make the life of a British soldier happy wether it be at home or abroad, everything has been done for you to lead strong and healthy lines, you are surrounded with all kinds of sports material which you are expected to use. a lot of your increases in pay entirely depends upon your efficiency, and only one way to do that is to safe guard your health when your health fails so does yours efficiency and automatically your pay drops. Temptations you will find plenty especially abroad which once indulged in is very hard to break, keep away from the native women with whom you come in contact with, many a promising young soldiers career has been cut short through these women my advice to you is to avoid them like poison. contagious deseases caught from these women is ten thousand times worse than that contrasted from european women, another thing to avoid is their native intoxicating drink, which has a far different action upon the human body than that to what you have been used to. dont think this is all bunk, it is perfectly true, I have seen this with my own eyes, and is good sound advice which I hope you will follow. This was one of a serious of lectures that often took place in the afternoons, other lectures were on different subjects such as the Advantages of the army, care and management of the rifle, memorising the names of the component parts etc What and what not to do in face of enemy fire and a hundred and one other things all to do with the army

Appendix C

Army Discipline

As soon as a recruit fixed his signature to his attestation papers, he immediately came under the iron discipline of the rigid military law of the British Army and was subject to punishment according to the offense he committed. With the exception of a very few cases, he was outside the jurisdiction of the civil authorities.

There were two forms of punishment awarded to soldiers, commonly known as CB and cells. CB or confinement to barracks for a number of days was awarded for minor offenses such as being absent without leave or for neglecting to obey the order of some NCO. Cells were awarded for more serious offenses, such as striking or threatening to strike an NCO or commissioned officer. The punishment might range from a few hours' detention to a number of years at hard labour in some military prison, usually located in the vicinity of the military boundaries. Cells could only be dealt out by a commanding officer of the unit, a camp commandant in charge of a number of regimental details of the camp, or some senior officers not under the rank of major. There was of course a limit to what even those officers couldn't go beyond in punishing offenders. There were of course several forms of court-martial, the highest known as general court-martial, which has the power to send a man to prison for life, and in the case of being on active service might order a soldier to be shot.

The lieutenant of a company had the power, in the absence of a more senior officer, to confine a soldier to barracks for no longer than three days. A captain of a company could award seven days, but if he considered the crime too serious for his judgment, he remanded the man to be tried by his commanding officer, who had the power to send the offender to prison for not more than 168 hours. Crimes warranting more severe punishment were tried by some form of court-martial determined by the nature and seriousness of the offense committed.

Drunkenness in the Army was usually met with a fine, accompanied with a few days CB for the first three offenses, after which the fine automatically became a court-martial offense and could be met by a prison sentence and discharge from the Army. Drunkenness in the Army was winked at unless it was accompanied by some more serious crime such as violence. Some men could adapt themselves more readily than others to the disciplinary measures of the Army. Then again, some never could and never would. Consequently, desertions frequently occurred. Many old soldiers hung on and wouldn't be kicked out.

Upon joining up, a soldier had to be in his barracks room by ten p.m., lights had to be out at 10:15 p.m., but after a few weeks he was permitted to be absent from barracks until midnight, providing he had no duties to perform. Five minutes after midnight, he'd forfeit that privilege and also get a few days' CB. Very seldom an excuse was taken for granted, so strict were the regulations. There were numerous other little offenses, such as having hair a little too long, or a man might neglect to shave himself, all of which was a military crime and was punished accordingly. Then there was the rigid inspection on certain parades. A soldier's buttons or boots might not be sufficiently polished, his rifle might have a few specks of dust on it, and several other minor complaints might be found with him, and of course he had to be punished. All the Army's little things got under the skin of the newly born recruit, but if he successfully braved all those small affairs for a couple of years, he began to find life as a soldier much more comfortable.

On one occasion, a regiment of soldiers was returning to barracks after a hard field day, and none of them appeared to be in a very cheerful mood. As was usual, upon the regiment's entering the barracks, the band struck up the regimental march; the CO on horseback stood by as the companies marched past him. The customary "eyes right" was ordered, and one soldier who had his head turned to the right failed to look into the CO's face. The CO ordered him arrested, and of course he had to be punished. The rules and regulations of the British Army had to be obeyed, but who would have thought the eagle eyes of that CO could detect such a fault in a regiment of soldiers marching past him in columns of fours? Those were a few of the things which went into the making of a soldier of the British Army.

The military prison, although spotlessly clean, was an institution which no soldier wanted to see a second time. The old saying still applied that "they can tame lions within the walls," and rather than go back for a second dose, many men had taken to desertion. Once inside, everything had to be done at the double. To the toilet he had to run, same thing to the wash house and back again. If he had a rusty pan to shine, he had to do it on the run. He had to run in full marching order for one hour at a time. The physical exertions he had to go through were enough to kill a lion. So much stonebreaking has to be done on time, and when he was locked up in his cell for the night, he had so much oakum to pick before lights out, and woe betide him if his task wasn't finished before the morning. Some of those fellows who had found their way into military prisons were hardened criminals, but they would rather see the inside of a civil jail than a military detention barracks. The wardens were hard-disciplined NCOs, selected for their harshness and firmness in dealing with prisoners. A man could expect no mercy from them in no form whatsoever. The chief might be anything from a captain up to a colonel who didn't hesitate to mete out extra punishment on the least complaint of a warden.

The only consolation a prisoner got might be from the prison chaplain, and even his visits were restricted in terms of time. The food might be good but by no means wholesome and certainly not sufficient to maintain a person who had to perform such manual labour. Porridge with salt for breakfast, weak soup and bread for dinner. Supper consisted of dry bread and water; sometimes, a little weak tea was served. There were no concessions, however, for good conduct. Obedience was first, last, and always in the British Army. "Obey first and complain afterwards" was the order.

Appendix D

Glossary

A-1 men: men who are first class; excellent

ADC: Aide de Camp

anna: "a copper coin formerly used in India and Pakistan" (*The American Heritage Dictionary of the English Language*, 3rd ed.) equal to 1/16 rupee

arrack: "a strong alcoholic drink of the Middle East and the Far East, usually distilled from fermented palm sap, rice, or molasses" (*The American Heritage Dictionary of the English Language*, 3rd ed.)

B1: type of steamer

babu: a Hindu clerk literate in English

baksheesh: tipping, charitable giving

bellam: a type of gondola, 30 to 40 feet long; light canoe

beriberi: "a nervous system ailment caused by a thiamine deficiency (deficiency of vitamin B_1) in the diet . . . often caused by eating polished white rice (milled rice that has had its husk, bran, and germ removed [and its thiamine])"; white rice was preferred by the middle class (*Wikipedia*)

blimey: an exclamation of surprise

BSMR: Bisanattam Railway—in India

"buckled to": to prepare rigorously, especially for battle; a metaphor for buckling armor (*Imperial Dictionary of the English Language*)

"bull ring": a place where British soldiers would get together with prostitutes; part of the bazaar

bullock: a castrated bull; a steer

bullocks carts: carts pulled by one or more bullock

bully beef: tinned corn beef

bund: an embankment or dike

cantonments: temporary or semipermanent military quarters (*Wikipedia*)

CB: confined to barracks

charpoy: a type of Indian mat or couch; British for "bed"

chats: a mineral ore used to filter water (*Imperial Dictionary of the English Language*)

chit: note or receipt

"climbed down a peg": lost a bit of superiority

CO: commanding officer

crown: British coin worth one dollar American money

demi: a small auxiliary engine

dhow: a one-masted Arab boat

"don't yer know": slang term for a condescending, arrogant British officer

"dumplins'": reference to Norfolk soldiers

echelon formation: "a formation of troops in which each unit is positioned successively to the left or right of the rear unit to form a oblique or steplike line" (*The American Heritage Dictionary of the English Language*, 3rd ed.)

embark: to go aboard a ship; from the Spanish *embarcar*

embarkation: "the act of going aboard a vessel . . . , as at the start of a journey" (*The American Heritage Dictionary of the English Language*, 3rd ed.)

embursements: advancements; loans

entrain: to get on a train

"eyes right": military drill command ordering individuals to turn their heads right (*Wikipedia*)

fakirs: Indian fortune tellers

"fall in": to take one's place in a military formation

French leave: an informal, unannounced, or abrupt departure

gharry: a horse-drawn cab

gharry-wallah: a gharry driver

GHQ: general headquarters

GIP: the Great Indian Peninsula railway, a British railway

GOC: general officer commanding

half a crown: 50 cents American money

in arrears: "the state of being behind in fulfilling obligations" (*American Heritage Dictionary*, 3rd ed.)

"in one's bad books": in one's bad opinion

John Barleycorn: personification of liquor

Jubbalpore: city in India, known as Jabalpur after India gained its independence from Britain

jug: slang for military prison; jail

junk: a Chinese flat-bottomed boat

Kelvin engine: diesel marine engine

"kick over the traces": slang phrase for getting out of military camp and "living it up"

"knuckle under": "to yield to pressure; give in" (*The American Heritage Dictionary of the English Language*, 3rd ed.)

last post: bugle call sounded at military funerals

lighter: "a type of flat-bottomed barge used to transfer goods and passengers to and from moored ships" (*Wikipedia*)

mahaila: Arab sail boat

March Royal: "Rule Brittania"

MFP: military foot police

miadan: a raised area/stage/gathering place in the middle of an Indian city

moll: a woman of questionable morals; a prostitute

MP: military police

natty: neat, trim and smart; dapper

NCO: noncommissioned officer

No. 1 field punishment: a World War I British Army punishment for minor offenses, such as drunkenness: "The soldier in question was attached standing full-length to a fixed object—either a post or a gun wheel—for up to two hours a day (often one hour in the morning and another in the afternoon) for a maximum of 21 days" (http://www.firstworldwar.com/atoz/fieldpunishment.htm)

nullah: "a ravine or gully, especially in Southern Asia" (*The American Heritage Dictionary of the English Language*, 3rd ed.)

oakum: loose hemp or jute fiber, used chiefly in caulking seams in wooden ships and in packing pipe joints

OC: officer commanding

P tents: generic term for different sizes of tents; e.g., 1-P tent (one-person tent), 2-P tent (two-person tent), etc.

parapet: "an earthen or stone embankment protecting soldiers from enemy fire—synonymous to bulwark" (*The American Heritage Dictionary of the English Language*, 3rd ed.)

peg: British slang for a drink of liquor

pence (pl. of penny): a coin used in Great Britain at the time of WWI, worth 1/12 of a shilling or 1/240 of a pound

pice (pl)/pica(s): a monetary unit worth 1/64 of a rupee used in India at the time of WWI

picquets: guards who stand at the edge of camp and watch for the enemy

playbook: a notebook containing descriptions and diagrams of the movement of soldiers

pound: "the basic monetary unit of the United Kingdom, worth 20 shillings; also called *pound sterling*" (*The American Heritage Dictionary of the English Language*, 3rd ed.)

"present arms": "a position in the military manual of arms in which the rifle is held vertically in front of the body; a command to assume "present arms" or to salute" (*The American Heritage Dictionary of the English Language*, 3rd ed.)

Pte: private

putties: a piece of white cloth wrapped spirally around the leg from the ankle to the knee

ration chip: note or receipt turned in to get rations

RE: Royal Engineers

RIM: Royal Indian Marine

RIN: Royal Indian Navy

roll call: "the reading aloud of a list of names of people, as in . . . a military post, to determine who is present or absent" (*The American Heritage Dictionary of the English Language*, 3rd ed.)

"rum": British slang for odd or strange

rupee: basic unit of Indian currency; at the time of WWI, 15 rupees equaled 1 British pound

"sahib": "used . . . as a form of respectful address for a European man in colonial India" (*The American Heritage Dictionary of the English Language*, 3rd ed.)

"salaam": "a ceremonial act of deference or obeisance, especially a low bow performed while placing the right palm on the forehead; a respectful ceremonial greeting performed especially in Islamic countries" (*The American Heritage Dictionary of the English Language*, 3rd ed.)

Sam Browne belt: combination of a pistol belt and shoulder strap (and D-rings) . . . the strap was intended to help carry the weight of a heavy pistol or sword. Named for General Sir Sam Browne of the British Army in India (http://www.diggerhistory.info/pages-uniform/Sam_browne.htm)

sand rats: British soldier slang for low-rate prostitutes

sappers: equivalent to private soldiers in the Royal Engineers. Originally, diggers of *saps*: a listening post in no man's land, connected at ninety degrees to the fire trench by a narrow communication trench. During an advance, saps were often joined together to make the new front line trench (from "WWI; an almost forgotten language" www.diggerhistory.info/pages-slang/ww1.htm)

serang: an unlicensed crew member on a boat

short-arm inspection: military slang for medical inspection of male's genitals for signs of sexually transmitted diseases (*Wikipedia*)

shoey: nickname for the shoeing smith

shilling: "a coin used in the United Kingdom, worth $^{1/20}$ of a pound" (*The American Heritage Dictionary of the English Language*, 3rd ed.)—about 25 cents in American money

shy pilot: nickname for parson

slope arms: "Individuals place the rifle in the slope, which is with the magazine and pistolgrip facing to the individual's left, and the rifle resting on the left shoulder, supported by the left arm at an angle of ninety degrees." (*Wikipedia*, "Drill Terms")

spine pads: "a flannel 'spine pad' that was supposed to reduce incidents of heatstroke by protecting the spine from the sun" *Hell in the Holy Land: World War I in the Middle East* by David R. Woodward, p. 88. University Press of Kentucky, 2006.

sovereign: a gold coin used in Great Britain at the time of WWI

SS: abbreviation for "ship"

Swede: British slang for rutabaga

T boat: small boat with a T-shaped top, providing shade and protection from rain

T3: a type of steamer

tattoo: "a signal sounded on a drum or bugle to summon soldiers . . . to their quarters at night" (*The American Heritage Dictionary of the English Language*, 3rd ed.)

toddy trees: a species of palm tree; from 15-year-old trees is harvested sweet sap—when fermented in the sun, it becomes an alcoholic drink

Tommies: slang for British soldiers (not officers)

tonga: "a light horse-drawn carriage used for transportation in India" (*Wikipedia*)

"top hole": British slang for first rate, the best

topi: a pith helmet worn for protection against the sun and heat

tot(s): a drink/drinks

Twin Canals: a small camp close to the rear of the lines

Union Jack: British flag

yard square: British equivalent to American "square yard"

CPSIA information can be obtained
at www.ICGtesting.com
Printed in the USA
FFOW01n1415240114
3229FF